Praise for *It's Called Work for a Reason!*

"With a writing style best described as full-throttle rant, the host of the A&E reality show *Big Spender* reveals the naked truth about careers. . . . Winget sets a high threshold for delivering a likeable, useful book that will educate and promote behavioral changes. Yet he delivers. His brutal frankness about what's wrong with how businesses—big and small—operate offers a refreshing contrast to other career counseling and management books. . . . His advice is solid: delivering results is the most fulfilling career move one can make." —*Publishers Weekly*

"[Winget's] advice . . . is so blunt and so true that it might keep you sane until you retire." —*Bloomberg News*

"His clear sense of personal integrity and ethics are a much needed refresher in today's business climate." —*BookPage*

"Winget is a no-holds-barred professional guru who . . . [offers] no-nonsense solutions about how to fix the problem." —*Pages*

"Larry Winget simultaneously takes on everyone from smart-ass employees and motivational speakers to bad service, bad sales-people, and bad bosses. It's not a fair fight. Winget has an unfair advantage—he tells the truth and doesn't give a damn if you like it or not. But like it or hate it, Larry will challenge you to be as amazing as you know you are."
—Joe Calloway, author of *Work Like You're Showing Off!*

"Thin skinned? No sense of humor? Don't read this book! I warned you. On the other hand, if you want to read a book that cuts through the normal fluff and challenges you personally, then pay attention: Larry Winget will irritate you to be a better employee and a better person."
—Mark Sanborn, C.S.P., C.P.A.E.; president of Sanborn & Associates, Inc.; and author of *The Fred Factor*

Kelly Campbell

Larry Winget, aka The Pitbull of Personal Development®, is the author of *You're Broke Because Want to Be* and the *Wall Street Journal* bestseller *Shut Up, Stop Whining and Get a Life*. One of the country's leading business speakers and a member of the National Speakers Association Hall of Fame, he gives approximately one hundred speeches per year to businesses and organizations around the country, sharing his insights and principles in the areas of success, leadership, customer service, and sales. Larry is also the host of A&E's reality series *Big Spender*, in which he coaches families in financial crisis. He lives in Paradise Valley, Arizona, with his wife, Rose Mary; his French bulldog, Butter; and his cat, Sparky Bob.

It's Called
WORK
for a Reason!

Your Success Is Your Own Damn Fault

Larry Winget

GOTHAM
BOOKS

GOTHAM BOOKS
Published by Penguin Group (USA) Inc.
375 Hudson Street, New York, New York 10014, U.S.A.

Penguin Group (Canada), 90 Eglinton Avenue East, Suite 700, Toronto, Ontario, Canada
M4P 2Y3 (a division of Pearson Penguin Canada Inc.); Penguin Books Ltd, 80 Strand,
London WC2R 0RL, England; Penguin Ireland, 25 St Stephen's Green, Dublin 2, Ireland (a
division of Penguin Books Ltd); Penguin Group (Australia), 250 Camberwell Road,
Camberwell, Victoria 3124, Australia (a division of Pearson Australia Group Pty Ltd);
Penguin Books India Pvt Ltd, 11 Community Centre, Panchsheel Park, New Delhi–110 017,
India; Penguin Group (NZ), 67 Apollo Drive, Rosedale, North Shore 0632, Auckland, New
Zealand (a division of Pearson New Zealand Ltd); Penguin Books (South Africa) (Pty) Ltd, 24
Sturdee Avenue, Rosebank, Johannesburg 2196, South Africa

Penguin Books Ltd, Registered Offices: 80 Strand, London WC2R 0RL, England

Published by Gotham Books, a member of Penguin Group (USA) Inc.

Previously published as a Gotham Books hardcover edition, January 2007

First trade paperback printing, January 2008

10 9 8 7 6 5 4

Gotham Books and the skyscraper logo are trademarks of Penguin Group (USA) Inc.

The trademarks for The Pitbull of Personal Development® and The World's Only
Irritational Speaker® are owned by Larry Winget.

THE LIBRARY OF CONGRESS HAS CATALOGED THE HARDCOVER EDITION AS FOLLOWS:

Winget, Larry.
    It's called work for a reason! : your success is your own damn fault / by Larry Winget.
        p. cm.
    ISBN: 978-1-592-40226-7 (hardcover)   ISBN: 978-1-592-40281-6 (paperback)
    1. Success in business.   2. Self-actualization (Psychology)   I. Title.
HF5386.W59 2007
650.1—dc22
2006025388

Printed in the United States of America
Set in Janson Text with Solstice   •   Designed by Sabrina Bowers

Contents

Preface

Before you start this book, you need a word of warning.

There will be parts of this book you won't like.

Why would I say that? Why would any author begin his book by telling his readers they won't like it? Because you will find out soon enough anyway, and I think you should be forewarned.

I would rather just tell you up front that my book is going to contain lots of stuff that will make you mad. Stuff that will bother you. Stuff that will be contrary to what you have become comfortable with. Contrary to what you believe. Stuff that will piss you off. Insult you.

Telling you all of this up front just seems more honest to me.

Now that we have that out of the way, can you tell already this book is not going to be your typical business book?

I hope so.

I have read thousands of business books. That is no exaggeration. I really have read thousands. All except a handful have been a total waste of time.

As a reader, I would have appreciated being warned that the business book I was about to read was nothing but worthless drivel. But they didn't warn me. The author let me read the entire book and find out page by page that it was full of meaningless information. Then when I was finished, I put the book down and was pissed off that I had just wasted my time reading a book that basically said very little and had no practical application.

Most of the authors of business books on the market today like to stroke people's egos by reinforcing information they already know. They tend to say, "You are really doing a good job; you just need to do it a little bit better or think slightly differently." Others give you a detailed statistical analysis of the economy or buying trends or another analytical detail that encourages you to get lost in the pages of boredom until you have no idea what the book is even about. Some authors exploit the hottest new buzzword of the day (think *branding*) and beat it to death, without giving you any real idea how to do what they suggest must be done. Some say that all you have to do is love your job in order to be successful at it. The worst of the lot tell cute little parables through inane dialogues, with messages so simple and trite that we should all be insulted. Business books contain too much jargon, too much cute, too much pie-in-the-sky, too much BS, too much of everything except the key ingredient to success in business: work!

All of those books are selling a load of crap. And people are lapping it up like ice cream. The bottom-line answer to every problem in business is this: People aren't working!!

Most employees are simply not doing a good job—in fact, they barely do their jobs at all. Workers are poorly trained, if trained at all. Customer service isn't just bad, it is atrocious. And companies tolerate it, holding no one responsible while blaming the stupidity of the customer or a bad economy instead of their employees and, ultimately, themselves. Sales results are down in most companies because the salespeople don't pick up the phone and actually talk to customers. Customer service is horrible because employees aren't working at serving their customers, and their managers don't care enough to do anything about it. Employees don't do their jobs because no one expects them to, and there are no real penalties for *not* doing their jobs.

In this book I will make the case that poor results are the result of poor performance. I will take on the issues of sales, customer service, leadership and management, team building, change, and working with others and will point the finger of blame exactly where it needs to be pointed—in your face.

This book is going to be different from any you have read before. I am going to give it to you straight, with no sugarcoating and no cute little parables. I am going to use words you are familiar with, because I talk like you do.

This is a very opinionated book. That's really all I have to offer: opinions. Opinions I have developed after years of real living, real working, real managing, real experience, and being *real* stupid. These opinions have worked for me in every area of my work experience. I believe they will work for you, too.

Why should you listen to me?

I know what I'm talking about. I grew up working at anything that paid a buck. I shoveled manure, trimmed trees, was one of the first male telephone operators in the Bell System, worked retail, sold, managed, and was the company president. I've been on the payroll and I've been responsible for making payroll. I've worked at just about every level of management and nonmanagement in both little bitty companies and in some of the largest companies on earth.

I was an award-winning salesperson and a top-ranked sales manager for AT&T. I started three companies from nothing and built them to be successful, thriving businesses. I've worked with and spoken to nearly four hundred of the Fortune 500 companies. I've traveled the world, speaking to every kind of business organization and association imaginable. I am a member of the International Speaker Hall of Fame. I am the host of a television show, helping people who made financial disasters of their lives. Impressed yet? It doesn't matter. Just know this:

I've worked for big companies, and I've managed and owned small companies. I did a lot of things right along the way. I have also made every stupid mistake anyone can make in business. I have lost sales, delivered bad customer service, treated employees poorly, been lazy . . . the works. I've even gone bankrupt and lost it all. If it can be done wrong, I have done it. I could be the poster child for stupidity in business.

I am not a professor of economics and I don't have a Ph.D. in business. I am a regular guy who came up the hard way, with lots of hard work. I learned some stuff along the way. I talked to people smarter than I was to learn from their experiences. I read more than three thousand books, some horrible and some priceless, so I could figure out what works and what doesn't work. I listened to more than five thousand hours of audio from the best business minds around and got every morsel of good information I could from them. I studied, listened, and experimented until I figured out what it took to be successful. I went from bankrupt to multimillionaire as a result.

I now travel the world, speaking to businesspeople about how to be more successful. I talk to people in the trenches—the people who really do the work. I work with managers, franchise owners, and front-line supervisors who are desperate for some straight talk on how to do a little better. I talk to white-collar, blue-collar, and no-collar employees who aren't getting what they need from anyone else. They pay me to tell them what to do. That's what you are doing when you buy this book, paying me to give you some usable advice on how to be more successful. I want you to get your money's worth.

"How do I know this book is for me, Larry?"

If you get a paycheck, this book is for you.

It's for you if you work for a living, have ever worked for a living, or ever plan on working for a living. It is for the kid straight out of college about to start her first real job to the CEO who has been around for fifty years. It is for the secretary, the salesperson, the stock clerk, and the janitor. I have written this book for anyone who has a job—whether you manage others or others manage you.

This book contains some answers. Not all of the answers, for sure! I would never pretend to have all of the answers. These are just the answers to problems I have faced in business.

These ideas are the things that have personally worked for me. I won't ask you to do anything that I haven't done myself. If my ideas make sense to you, then try them to see if they work. If they work for you, then celebrate, because it's all been worth it. If my ideas don't make sense to you, I suggest you try them anyway. After all, what you are currently doing probably isn't working so well and you are probably ready for something new. If you try my ideas and they don't work, what have you really lost? A little time, a little effort, and a little money. But you will still be one step closer to knowing what is right for you.

As you read this book, you may be prone to say, "I know this stuff." I hope you do! I can't imagine where you have been hiding if you haven't become familiar with the concepts of taking personal responsibility, doing what you are paid to do, having personal integrity, using common sense, doing the right thing, and making tough decisions. That's the crux of my book. No brain surgery involved. Just a handful of simple ideas we should all be reminded of and shown how to use in every situation. These ideas are perfect for anyone in any business. But they are more than just business ideas. These are ideas for life.

So let's get started. Let me beat you up, tick you off, and possibly teach you something along the way. Be open to finding one good idea. Yes, just one. There is no shortage of good ideas here, but my goal is that you find a good idea that you will put to use immediately. One good idea can change your life, change your business, and make you rich. If you got only one good idea from this book, wouldn't it be worth the price you paid for it? Of course it would. So start reading. Get a highlighter and a pen and start marking up the book as you go. Find your one good idea and get started on it today!

"People would rather be nice than right, rather be sensitive than be true. Well, being nice and sensitive are important, but they're not more important than being right; they're not more important than the truth." —BILL MAHER

It's Called

WORK

for a Reason!

CHAPTER 1

"Hi-ho, hi-ho, it's off to work I go . . ."

"Bye, honey, I'm going to work!"

Oh, bull! You aren't going to work at all. You are going to that place that isn't home, where you have to dress a little better than you do around the house. You are going to the place that is full of other people who also just lied to their significant others when they said they were going "to work." You are all liars—you and those people you say you work with. You say you are coworkers, when the truth is you are only co-goers.

Most studies say that people actually work only about half of the time they are on the job. And don't ask me to cite to those studies—I didn't actually have time to do the work to find the studies. I was too busy goofing off. You know about goofing off, don't you? You do it about half the time you are "at work." But I

1

have heard about those studies, and they almost all say that people work only about half the time. The rest of the time is spent socializing, eating, griping, writing e-mails, surfing the Web, drinking coffee, daydreaming, going to the bathroom more than you need to, and stretching every break from fifteen minutes to twenty-five minutes and lunch hour to seventy-five minutes. This translates into a 50 percent effort from 100 percent of the employees. And the reason it goes by unchecked is because every single person in the company is doing it—from the janitor to the CEO.

When everyone works half the time, it takes twice as many people to do the work. That translates to higher payroll expenses, higher insurance costs, higher taxes, and higher prices. The high cost of doing business is the result of lazy people not working.

Reality check: It's called *work* for a reason!

It's not called playtime. It's not called socializing time. It's called work. Sadly, most employees don't seem to understand this concept. Schools don't teach it. Kids aren't taught it at home. It isn't made clear to new employees. It isn't enforced. It isn't really expected. It isn't managed. The example isn't there. It is only griped about when it doesn't get done.

You were hired to WORK

What is work? Being productive. Getting results. That's why they hired you. You are there to generate more revenue for the company than you cost the company. Your contribution must outweigh your expense. You do that not by dilly-dallying around but by doing the assigned tasks in a fast, efficient, cost-effective way. You do that by being proficient at doing the right things. You will know you are doing a good job when you are tired from doing it. You will know you are working when you break a sweat—either physically or mentally. Got it?

You aren't working as hard as you think you are. Like most people, you work just hard enough so they won't fire you, and they pay you just enough so you won't quit.

Your company isn't working as hard as its annual report says. It gives lip service to customer service but doesn't really deliver it. It says "We are making every effort to . . ." when what it really means is "we're having meetings about it and sending out memorandums regarding it."

Face it: Productivity sucks. Want me to prove it? What have you accomplished today? Seriously. What have you done that actually contributes to the bottom line of the organization that writes you a check? Don't lie. Don't fool yourself. Just tell yourself the truth. You are the only one who will know right now, so go ahead and ask, "What have I done today?" Go ahead and do it now, I've got time. What have you done?

Now, cut it by 75 percent and you will be closer to the real truth about what you have actually done.

How does this happen?

We focus on process instead of accomplishment. We have become spectators instead of doers. We reward the wrong things.

We tolerate poor performance. We don't teach people how to be good workers. We don't create an environment that promotes work. Expectations are low. Enough reasons? Not really, but it's a good start. Let's look at them.

Incorrect focus

The best example of how we focus incorrectly is one of the most used items in business today. The To-Do List. Got one? Ever used one? Of course you have. It's a tool created to get people to focus and plan; yet it does just the opposite. Let me offer you a bit of Business Blasphemy: The To-Do List is a waste of time and is killing your productivity. Proof? Answer this question for me: What is more important, what you do or what you get done? Any semi-intelligent person will know that the correct answer is what you get done. But we don't focus on what gets done. We focus on what people are going to do. Let me ask you another question: What difference does it really make what people are doing as long as what needs to get done really gets done?

This question brings up other questions. Questions about leadership, management, productivity, performance reviews, quotas, and reward systems, just to name a few.

All employers love for their people to look busy. A manager can stand proudly with her boss and look out across a field of busy little bees and brag that her department is busy. Is that really important? Well, it is if customers can actually see people standing around doing nothing, because that would give a bad impression to customers. So in retail, the answer is yes, it is important for people to look busy. But if you work where customers can't see you, then I contend how busy you look is not always an accurate accounting of how much work has transpired. Don't measure busywork. Don't measure activity. Measure accomplishment. It doesn't matter what people do as much as it matters what they get done. The employee who looks busy all the time might actually accomplish the least. Yet the busy-appearing employee is typically the one who gets rewarded. Managers have to ignore appearances and look deeper at the work.

So here is what I suggest: Throw away the little tablets that say "Things to Do" at the top. Get rid of your leather-bound planner with the To-Do List on the left-hand side. Instead, get some "Things That Have to Get Done" pads printed. Yes, it's my idea and you should probably give me credit for it, but I am more interested in your getting things done. That way, when I call your company to ask about my order, you can just look at your list and happily reply with, "It's done." That is plenty of repayment for me.

"Oh, come on! What's the difference?"

While both types of lists are based on future performance, there is a huge difference between the mind-sets that the two different lists create. Your "Things to Do" list is not much more than a wish list. Your "Things That Have to Get Done" list is more focused and concise, and acts as an action plan for your day. It will force you to constantly evaluate your tasks and separate them into "what would be nice to do" and "what absolutely has to get done."

This is really what the whole concept of time management is about: doing what has to get done. But time management became something else over the years.

You don't have the time to manage your time. It's time consuming. Time spent managing time is time that should be spent doing other things—like getting the things done that have to get done.

Everyone should forget about managing time and should instead focus on managing priorities. When the right things get done, time takes care of itself.

The problem is that priorities are not clearly defined. Face it, if the most important thing gets done, what else really matters? The key is to know what the most important thing is.

"When priorities are clear, decision making is easy."

—ROY DISNEY

So what is the most important thing that has to get done in your business? Do you even know? If you don't, then you are wasting time, energy, and money. Every individual in the business has to know the most important thing that must be done every day.

"But, Larry, those things *and* others must all be done."

That's the problem. Lots of things should get done and yet

little of what absolutely has to get done actually gets done. What has to get done? Really *has* to get done? I didn't say "should get done" or "would be nice if that got done." I said "absolutely has to get done."

As soon as you know what has to get done, do it. It's as simple as that. Just do what absolutely has to get done. I didn't say you should do *only* that, but I did say do *that*. Do it first. Don't do anything else until it is done. Even if you have an overwhelming amount you would like to get done and it should be done, do what absolutely has to get done.

If that is the only thing you get done all day, you will be better off for having done it.

It really is that simple. Know your priorities.

Each job has priorities

A salesperson's priority is to make sales. What goes into making sales? Talking to customers. You normally can't sell something unless you ask someone to buy. That means the most important thing for any salesperson to do is to talk to customers and ask them to buy. Do salespeople have other things to do? Of course they do. They have to fill out their paperwork, turn in their orders, do follow-up within the company about their sales, and on and on and on. Those things all should be done. And they will get done. Right after the thing that absolutely must get done is done.

Every person's job has lots of things that must be done every day. I understand that. The problem is that we end up doing what we would like to get done, and that one thing that absolutely must get done just doesn't seem to get done. Why? There was no time to do it.

Well, bull. There is always enough time to do the one thing that must be done. That's why the "Things That Have to Get Done" list is so important. It will help you set your priorities and accomplish exactly what is critical to success.

We have become spectators instead of doers

People are no longer conditioned to work. They are conditioned to watch other people work. We have all become masters of observation. It is easier to watch *Friends* on TV than it is to have a friend or be a friend. It is easier to watch other people get a job on *The Apprentice* than it is to go find a job yourself. It's easier to be a big loser by sitting on your butt watching *The Biggest Loser* than it is to get off your butt and lose weight yourself. It's much more fun to watch someone on television painting her living room than it is to do it yourself. It is even easier to watch people on television use a TV nanny to discipline their kids than it is to discipline your own kids. So is it any wonder that when we come to work, we find it easier to watch others work than to do it ourselves? While this is a societal problem that has huge implications, in business it kills productivity and costs us all.

We reward the wrong things

We have a tendency to reward busy people for looking busy instead of getting things done. The guy who puts out very little effort yet accomplishes things rarely gets much recognition. People will label him as lucky or say that good things just fall in his lap. So? What if he really is lucky? What if good things really do just fall in his lap? What difference should that make? If he gets things done, he deserves the credit.

We reward people who come in early, stay late, and skip their lunch hours, all in the name of accomplishment. I wouldn't do this. If an employee can't figure out how to get her job done in the number of hours she is paid to work, it probably means she is goofing off when she is supposed to be working. Remember: It's not how many hours you put into the work, but how much work you put into the hours.

Am I saying that you should never come in early, stay late, or skip a lunch hour? Not at all. Sometimes you do whatever it takes to get the job done. But routinely, a job can be done in the number of hours for which you are paid. Don't reward someone for being a workaholic. It isn't healthy and it sends the wrong signals both to the workaholic and to other employees.

We tolerate poor performance

As a manager, you find it easier to turn your head and ignore a problem than it is to take the time to fix it. Big deal if someone is a little late; it's not worth writing them up for it or even talking to them about it. Why hassle them? Because they are late. They are paid to be there on time—not to be late.

Managers, get this straight: If you accept poor performance or let things slide, you are as guilty as the offending employee is. You are guilty by association. Guilty by acceptance. And your boss should discipline you for it. If he doesn't, then he is also guilty. He has become an accessory to the crime of poor performance.

We don't teach people how to be good workers

Companies spend more time disciplining a poor employee for doing the job wrong than they did teaching the employee to do it right. Most companies don't have a training budget, don't have time set aside to educate their employees, don't offer any training except "This is your job, do it."

We don't create an environment that promotes work

Offices are cluttered and disorganized. The front and back doors have become smoke-holes. You can dress like a hobo on Fridays because it's "casual day." The break room is always full of cake left over from celebrating someone's birthday. People eat at their desks.

Offices no longer look like places where work gets done. Instead, they look like places where slobs party.

Expectations are low; standards are lower

I have a friend who manages the shoe department at a major high-end department store. She told me not long ago that her biggest challenge was just to get people to actually come to work—and when they do, she is so happy to have warm bodies working the floor that she doesn't say that much about performance. She even related a story about an employee who, on his second day of work, went to lunch and didn't come back. He then showed up three days later for his shift and was amazed that he had been fired.

Employees don't perform well because they aren't expected to perform well. Their management is just happy they came to work, so how they deal with customers, make sales, work well with others, and learn the company's product line hardly enters into the picture.

Standards are lower than expectations. When you don't expect much, you don't get much. When you don't get much over a long period of time, performance standards drop.

Did you ever go to a great restaurant that in time became your favorite? You went there fairly often. The word got out and soon you couldn't even get a reservation there. Then one day it just wasn't as good as it once was. The service was a little slow, the water glass was a little dirty, and the food wasn't quite as good. You were unhappy but realized that everyone can have a bad day, so you returned a few weeks later, but again it wasn't like it used to be. You tried it one more time. A month later you drive by and there are four cars in the parking lot. Two months later a FOR LEASE sign is in front of the building. How did that happen? One day a manager let a mistake slide. He didn't correct it because he was too busy or didn't feel good, or it just wasn't worth the argument. So the employee got by with less than excellent performance. A couple of other employees noticed that the first guy didn't get in trouble for sloppy performance, so they deduced it was okay to do the same. The manager wasn't complaining and the customers weren't saying anything. At that point, poor performance became standard performance. The manager might have mentioned it to the employees and perhaps their response was that the first guy got by with it, so what was the problem? Regardless, it didn't get fixed and excellence slipped into mediocrity. Before you know it, everyone is out of a job.

One little slip and the whole place goes under. Extreme? Maybe . . . but maybe not. It takes time, that's for sure. But the organizations that refuse to accept poor performance at any level and that take the time to deal with every slip in service do well regardless of economic conditions. They thrive in spite of it all just because they expect, demand, and deliver excellence at every level.

Is it tough to pull off? Of course it is. That's why so few do it. But it's what you were hired to do and what you are paid to do every day. Not doing it means you are stealing money from your employer by not giving them what they paid you to do. In other words . . .

You are a thief!

"What? How dare you call me a thief! You don't even know me!"

Sure I do. I know you well enough without ever having met you to tell you that every day, you steal.

While you are probably not stealing money from the cash register or embezzling funds from the big account or even swiping paper clips and Post-it notes, I can still guarantee you are a low-down, dirty thief. Any time you don't give your best effort, you are stealing. You steal from your company, because they paid you for your best effort. You steal from your coworkers, because they have to pick up your slack. You steal from your customers, because they pay retail for your best effort. Most of all, you steal from yourself.

Answer these questions honestly:

Do you knowingly stretch your coffee break and lunch hour
for longer than the allotted time?

Do you ever give a project less than your best effort?

Do you ever tell a little fib about how busy you were,
when in truth you were slacking off?

Are you ever guilty of giving your customers less than great service?

Do you ever take the "easy" road instead of the "right" road?

Do you ever call in sick when really you just wanted a day off?

If you answer yes to even one of these questions, you are a thief. And while all of us are guilty of some of these types of offenses from time to time, letting any of these slide will lead to a habit of mediocrity instead of excellence.

Think no one notices? It doesn't matter. Because even if they don't, you will know. You will know that you didn't do your best. You will know that you got paid for effort you didn't give. And you will eventually suffer the consequences. Guilt, resentment, poor evaluations, and more will surface. Most important, you won't feel good about yourself, because you won't have given your best. That will take its toll on your self-esteem and, ultimately, your performance.

"So what's the fix?"

Read on, brothers and sisters!

Larry's short list on how to work:

- *Stop lying to yourself and everyone else about how hard you work.*
- *Work faster, smarter, and harder. Stay busy. Find things to do.*
- *Stop periodically during the day and ask yourself: Does this matter? Is it contributing to the overall well-being of the company? Am I really getting something done or just killing time?*
- *Never tolerate poor performance in yourself or others.*
- *Create a clean, organized environment that encourages work.*
- *Expect the best from everyone.*
- *Teach your employees how to be good workers.*
- *Manage priorities, not time.*
- *Figure out what absolutely has to get done, and then do it first.*
- *Never get bogged down with the should-get-done's or the wouldn't-it-be-nice-to-get-done's or the easy-to-do's.*
- *There is plenty of time to do the right thing.*

"Opportunity is missed by most people because it is dressed in overalls and looks like work." —Thomas A. Edison

CHAPTER 2

Success is simple

Success is simple. It may not always seem that way, but I can promise you, it is. I doubt you were told that when you were growing up. You were probably told that success was complicated. That was a lie. After all of the time I have spent researching success and living the principles I learned along the way, I have yet to discover anything that was really complicated. When I read the biographies of the most successful people who ever lived, I find that none followed a complicated plan to achieve success. Success just isn't complicated.

Yet we all want success to be complicated. Now you may be saying, "Not me! I want it easy. I would love for success to be simple." That is also a lie. You don't really want success to be simple. You may say you do and even think you do, but you don't. You want it to be complicated so you will have an excuse for not doing well. And if you can convince others that success is complicated, then they will forgive you for not doing well.

Let's get this straight: There is no excuse for not doing well.

And I won't forgive you for not doing well. Others might, but I won't, because I know better. So does any other successful person. Life and business are profoundly simple. Not easy, but simple. There is a big difference. Success is never easy. If it were, there would be many more successful people in the world. Success is hard. It comes from hard work, staying focused, becoming excellent, and consistently delivering excellence, discipline, study, and much more. Those concepts are not complicated; they are simple ideas that require only hard work.

Good news

You understand the complicated stuff. I've met very few people who didn't get the complicated stuff. People are given a job. Then somehow they learn to do the job. They learn the cash register, the computer, and the mechanics of how to do every aspect of the job. At that point, they start to skip the simple things like showing up on time, or even showing up at all. They don't treat others with respect. They don't return phone calls. They don't keep appointments, and on and on and on. It's always the simple stuff we mess up. Do I sound like a broken record yet? I certainly hope so. I am unforgiving about this stuff. I am so sick of people complaining about how bad business is when the truth is:

Business isn't bad.

People are just bad at being in business.

There are no secrets

Speakers, trainers, and authors love to tell you that there are se-crets to success. When they have convinced you that there are secrets to being more successful, selling more, or being rich, they will convince you that only *they* possess those secrets. If you will give them your money, they will share those secrets with you. What a rip-off. Those people should be ashamed. (Not ashamed for trying to sell you their ideas, because we all have the right to do that. I sold you my ideas when you bought this book, so I have no problem with selling ideas.) They should be ashamed for saying there are secrets to being more success-ful. There are no secrets. There is no new information. The same things it takes to be successful today are the same things it has taken to be successful throughout history. I have discovered there are only a handful of good ideas in the whole world. You already know them. You have heard them your entire life. Here are some of the main keys to being more successful:

Take personal responsibility.

Things change, so be flexible.

Work smart and work hard.

Serve others well.

Be nice to others.

Be optimistic.

Have goals; want something big for yourself.

Stay focused.

Keep learning.

Become excellent at what you do.

Trust your gut.

When in doubt, take action.

Earn all you can. Save all you can. Give all you can.

Enjoy all you've got.

Above all: keep it simple!

Did you see any big secrets in my list? I hope not. But oh, how we love our little secrets! People will spend big money to hear a secret! I just checked Amazon.com and found there are more than thirty-nine thousand books listed with the word "secrets" in the title. Are there really that many secrets?

There are nearly 1,800 books about the secrets of success. Is it any wonder that people aren't doing well? They are confused! Success is not a secret—it never has been. There are only a few really good ideas and not one of them is a secret. I just gave them to you and my little list didn't even take up a full page, much less 1,800 books.

There are more than five hundred books about the secrets of customer service. How about trying this: Be nice. Is it much more complicated than that? Isn't that what we are all looking for? Someone to take our money and be nice to us?

There are more than six hundred books about the secrets of selling. How about this: Ask. Is that a secret in the world of selling? It must be, because there are more than six hundred books written about that big secret.

There are nearly seven hundred books listed about the secrets of leadership. You can find the secrets of leadership according to Attila the Hun, Santa Claus, Billy Graham, Jesus, Hitler, Queen Elizabeth, Saint Paul, Harry Potter, the Benedictine Monks, *Star Trek*, and the Bible. Every military leader of record seems to have secrets to share, along with most religious leaders and presidents. There are books that talk about the seven secrets, the eleven secrets, and the four secrets. Figure it out, people! How many leadership secrets are there? Here's an idea to try: Lead. Get out in front of your people and give them something to follow—just lead!

Stop the insanity!

Don't ever let anyone tell you that success in any area of life or business is complicated. Use your head. When it starts feeling complicated, just stop. Stop and evaluate what you are doing. Ask yourself why it seems to be so hard. Ask yourself if there is any way that you can drop some steps out of the process. Ask yourself if what you are doing is just busywork or whether you are really moving closer to your goals. Ask yourself if Santa Claus or Harry Potter really has much to teach you.

I keep it simple. Very simple. In this book I'll tell you what I think, give you a few pages about why I think it, tell you a good story or two, and then summarize it all into a handful of bullet points. If a person can't summarize his thoughts on success in business into a handful of bullet points, he doesn't know what he's talking about. And he's scamming you. Don't be a sucker.

You are smart enough to recognize BS when you see it. You are smart enough to know what makes sense and what doesn't.

That's why I want to warn you of some overlap in this book as you go from topic to topic. There are just a handful of basic life principles that I will be repeating a lot. What it takes to be successful in life is the same as what it takes to be successful in business. It works in the areas of selling, leadership, and customer service, whether you are an employee or the employer. What's good for the janitor is good for the CEO. So you will see my basic principles repeated from topic to topic. Don't say, "This guy is a broken record." I know I am. I've already told you that I don't believe any of this is all that hard, so what would you think if I gave you hundreds of different concepts for each topic? It all comes down to a handful of simple ideas that will work for anyone, at any time and in any situation.

The simple equation for business success

I go to approximately one hundred annual conventions and business meetings every year. Those meetings are full of general sessions, breakout sessions, luncheons, and banquets. Those meetings sometimes cost hundreds of thousands of dollars to put on. Every one of those meetings has one purpose: to make the business better. I like to be the opening speaker at these meetings just to dispel that misconception. I like to get their meeting started off right by telling them that their business isn't going to get any better because of the meeting. Businesses don't just get better, and they certainly won't because of a meeting. Businesses get better only when the people in the business get better.

That's the equation.

> *Business gets better right after the people in the*
> *business get better.*

That one simple equation works in every area of business.

> *Sales get better right after salespeople get better.*
>
> *Customer service gets better right after the people who deliver*
> *the customer service get better.*
>
> *Employees get better right after their manager gets better.*
>
> *Everything in your life gets better when you get better, and*
> *nothing is ever going to get better until you get better.*

See how simple that it is?

Larry's short list for keeping it simple:

- *If it starts feeling complicated, stop and reevaluate. There is a simpler way—find it.*
- *Stop listening to those who want to complicate things.*
- *Take action quickly on the simple ideas.*
- *There are no "secrets" to being more successful.*
- *Get better, and the things around you will get better.*
- *The things it takes to be successful in life are the same things it takes to be successful in business.*

CHAPTER 3

No one owes you a living

"Don't go around saying the world owes you a living; the world owes you nothing; it was here first." —Mark Twain

Chances are, the business where you work was there first too. The business was probably doing quite well before you got there, and it will still be doing quite well long after you are gone. So they don't really owe you much.

I once had a receptionist who insisted on doing personal things at her desk during work hours. Things like balancing her checkbook, doing her nails, talking to friends on the telephone, even having her friends come to the office to visit with her during work hours. When I confronted her with the problem, she told me that it was her desk and what she did at her desk was her business, not mine. She actually said to me that she was entitled to do whatever she wanted to do at her desk. Easy fix! Thirty seconds later it was no longer her desk.

Employees have developed a sense of entitlement regarding their jobs, their work space, and their company. Many people have become so dependent on their company, on society, and on others that they think they are owed a living. They think the company is there to serve them instead of the truth, which is that they are there to serve the company. They think that the employer is supposed to take care of every little aspect of their lives. Get a paper cut? File a medical claim. Someone flirt with you? Just file a harassment suit. And if the employer doesn't respond to this false sense of employee entitlement, they will likely find themselves defending a lawsuit.

All of this bothers me. Your company owes you a safe working environment. That's about it. As long as stuff doesn't fall on your head, the company has done its part. They don't owe you an environment in which you are safe from stupid people. Stupid people are everywhere, and while I hate that it's true, they just can't be legislated against. If that were the case, we would have to lock up the bulk of the workforce. Therefore, your bosses, your coworkers, and your customers will all say stupid things to you. You will be harassed. Your feelings will get hurt. You will stub your toe. It happens on the street and at home and you can't do a thing about it. It will also happen at work. It's called life.

Companies do not care about your feelings. They shouldn't have to. They should care about your rights. They will, for the most part, defend your rights. They don't have the time, the money, or the desire to make sure that you feel good about things. If you are happy on the job, that is a bonus. If you aren't happy, that's your fault and not the company's. You have been paid. Give thanks and move on.

The company doesn't exist to make you happy. They exist to make a profit so they can pay you so you can serve the customer well so the customer will keep paying for the company's services so they can remain profitable so they can pay you again. That is the cycle of business. Do your best to facilitate that cycle and don't bog it down with your sniveling.

In addition to a safe environment, you are owed a fair wage for a fair day's work. However, if you don't give a fair day's work, then I don't believe you are owed the fair day's wage. Somehow that very simple concept makes perfect sense to me. How does it elude so many others?

A deal is a deal

I am a big believer in the saying "A deal is a deal." When you and your employer decided that you were going to work together, you made a deal. The deal was you would show up when they told you to and you would do what they paid you to do. For that, you would receive an amount of money that you agreed to. A deal was struck and all agreed. That was probably just about all that was included. Of course there were details and some papers were probably signed—but I'll pretty much guarantee you that in the fine print on those forms you were signing they didn't promise that you would be happy. And they didn't promise that your coworkers were going to be perfect little angels who loved and adored you. And they didn't say that you wouldn't get tired or mad or sad or have your feelings hurt. You just struck a deal based on the work and the money. You provide the work and they provide the money.

The work ethic of our parents

What happened to the work ethic of our parents? They worked because they had jobs to do and because they took their commitments and their obligations seriously. They had been raised to believe that your word is your bond and that when you tell someone you will work, you work—with no argument. If someone hurts your feelings, oh well, that's part of the job. If someone makes you mad—again, that's just part of the job. If you get hurt, oh well, at least you have a job. If you work with idiots, deal with it. If your boss is an asshole, put up with it: he's the boss.

My dad worked for Sears for forty-seven years. He started when he was seventeen and got two years off to fight in World War II. He rarely missed work even when he was sick. He didn't always love it. He worked with, for, and around idiots every day, although I almost never heard him complain. He worked hard every day, coming home bone-tired at the end of the day. He worked in the warehouse for more than twenty years and then, after a washing machine fell on him, he was transferred inside the store to sell sporting goods. By the way, he didn't sue anyone when he got hurt on the job. He went to the hospital, got better, and went back to work. No hard feelings; stuff happens. Forty-seven years with one company. That's more than seventeen thousand days of showing up. And I will guarantee you that not one of those days did he ever think about whether he was going to have a happy day when he got there. He never once thought of motivation and attitude and his rights. His only motivation was to do the job he had been paid to do. Why? He had obligations. He had a family to take care of and bills to pay. But even more than that, he had made a deal with Sears when he was seventeen years old: You pay me and I'll work for you. Period. Not a complicated agreement. But one he believed in. He had personal integrity and he had made a commitment. He was proud of his job. In many people's eyes, it was a menial job. They give that job to idiots today. Don't believe me? Go into any major department store and prove it to yourself. But my dad took it seriously. He was on time, he worked hard while he was there, he gave good service because that was part of the job, and he did what he was told to do. Why? Because like it or not, happy or not, motivated or not, a deal is a deal. They paid—he worked.

"But, Larry, we've come a long way since then!"

You are right; we have come a long way. And in many cases, we have come too far. I am all for protecting people's rights. But damn, haven't we gone too far in favor of the employee's rights? Doesn't the company have rights, too?

Why should the company suffer because you aren't happy today? Why should I even care that you are having a bad day? The work is there whether you are in a bad mood or not. Customers still need to be served. Boxes still need to be shipped. The copier still needs to be fixed. Telephones still need to be answered. And if you are paid to do those things, then I expect you to do them. As your employer, I don't really need to concern myself with your happiness or your motivation. Besides, I have my own problems to deal with. I am a human with all the same problems you have. But mine also include making sure that the work gets done so the company is profitable enough to pay your salary.

What happened to you?

Why did you quit working? Wait, don't tell me . . . I don't care. It doesn't matter. It doesn't matter to me and it shouldn't to your employer, either. As long as they shell out the bucks every week, then you owe them the work that was agreed to in the original deal.

Always remember that you are an expense item to your company, and if you don't make yourself worth more than you cost, then you are an expense your company simply can't afford. You have become expendable. You can be made to go away and they will find someone else who will live up to the deal: someone who generates more value than he costs.

Pretend I'm your boss for a minute. Here is my position: Just do your damn job. And don't complain about it. And if you aren't willing to do that, then don't be surprised when I fire your lazy ass and tell you to get your butt out of my business.

Is that fair? Sure it is. It's fair to my customers. It's fair to the other employees who have to pick up the slack for your laziness. It's fair to me because I am the one paying you. And mostly, it's fair to you because I am rewarding you for the effort you are giving me. If you were my boss, I would think this arrangement made perfect sense.

Got it yet? No work—no pay. No work—no job.

"We've gotten to the point where everybody's got a right and nobody's got a responsibility."

—NEWTON MINOW, former chairman of the
Federal Communications Commission

Larry's short list for making a living:

- *Remember that you are not owed a living.*
- *A deal is a deal. Never forget it. Live by it.*
- *Remember the work ethic of our parents and our grandparents: They worked because they had a job to do and because they took their commitments and their obligations seriously.*
- *Make yourself worth more than you cost.*
- *Companies exist to make a profit, not to be sure you're happy.*
- *Accept responsibility for fixing your own problems.*

CHAPTER 4

Results are everything!

What are they paying you for?

"That's simple, Larry; they pay me to work hard!"

Funny how many people think that. In fact, you may think that is what I have been talking about in this book: working hard. Sorry, but that's wrong.

I like people who work hard. I admire hard work. But you are not paid to work hard. In fact, you are not paid for effort at all.

You are paid for results. It's not what you do; it's what you get done. Remember that "Things That Have to Get Done" list I talked about earlier? I warned you that concept would keep showing up.

Some people are able to achieve great results with very little effort. They make sales easily. Customers like them. They solve problems with ease. Yet there are others who have to work very hard and put in long hours and real sweat to achieve the same results.

As your employer, if I see that you have to work hard to get your results, yet your coworkers achieve their results with little effort, don't be surprised if I'm not all that impressed with your hard work.

And if you happen to be one of those people who have to work hard to get things done, I suggest that you not complain to me about your coworkers skating by and achieving good results. As your manager, I won't be on your side. Because I don't pay for effort, I pay for results.

Results are everything

We pretend that other stuff is important, but what really matters is results. They rarely ask how—they always ask how many. Everything else is a smoke screen. What exactly are your results? On a personal level, your results are your house, car, clothes, spouse, job, friends, health, happiness—whatever you have or are experiencing make up your results. On a business level, they are your office, your profits, your goodwill, your service to others and the community and your employees—whatever your company has or is experiencing makes up your company's results.

Never kid yourself about your results. It doesn't matter what your company brochure says or what your company slogan or mission statement is. What matters are the results these things produce.

Results are everything and they never lie.

Why are results so bad?

The number-one reason results aren't what they ought to be: APATHY.

People simply don't care. Employees don't care if they do a good job or a bad job. Their boss doesn't seem to care one way or another either. And it seems that no one cares about the customer. What's interesting is that most studies say that the number-one reason customers stop doing business with a company is because they don't feel anyone cares about them. Yet, even customers don't care enough to complain about it when they don't get good service, because they believe that no one cares and nothing will change even when they do complain. Employees don't care because many times they simply don't understand what there is to care about. We have reached the point where apathy is a way of doing business. Don't believe me? I don't care.

Even if an employee gets fired for not caring, there is another job waiting for him down the street and another poor schmuck who will gladly hire him. How does that happen? Easy. When the new employer calls the old employer for a reference, the old employer can't legally say anything bad about the person.

Bad employees can move from one job to another and employers have no way to hang together to assure that bad employees don't get hired. Does this make sense to you? I could get off on a serious rant here, but I'll save it for later.

One reason people don't care is that it hasn't been explained to them why they should care. No one has ever explained to them that treating the customer well, keeping the workplace clean, looking good, being polite, and working well with their fellow employees all add up to the company's being profitable. They don't understand that a profitable company is more likely to stay in business, which means that the employees can continue to reap the benefits they are accustomed to. Most employees have no idea when they receive $40,000 in salary, the company must pay another 40 percent in associated costs. This is excellent information to share with your employees. It might give them a new respect for pricing, service, sales, and the true cost of doing business.

As a business owner or manager, ask yourself this question: What do I pay my people for? The answer: results. Not time. Not attitude. Not enthusiasm. Just results.

My manager, Vic Osteen, is the perfect example of all of this. Vic runs everything. He runs the company; I don't. I have ideas, but it is up to Vic to make sure my ideas become reality. He handles all contact with clients, manages the other staff, works with the bureau that represents me, deals with all suppliers, and makes most of the business decisions about the day-to-day operations of the company. I trust him completely. I have empowered him to do whatever it takes to keep customers happy, to keep everyone in my company making money, and to keep me busy.

I own the company; Vic runs the company. I work for Vic.

I have no idea how much Vic works. I know he takes a lot of time off. He takes lots of canoe trips, bicycle trips, runs marathons, goofs off—sometimes it seems like he is gone more than he's there. Know what? I don't care. I notice, but I don't care. Why? The job I hired him to do always gets done, without exception. I don't care how many hours he puts in. If it takes him eighty hours to get it done or eight hours to get it done, it doesn't matter to me. I just care that it gets done. If he can get it done in eight hours, then good for him. If he can get it done in two hours, then better for him. If it takes him eighty hours to get it done, that's not really any of my concern. He should have worked either harder or smarter. I am also not interested in whether Vic's attitude is all that good or if he's having a bad day or not feeling well. I'm sorry and I wish him the best, but I am not paying him to be happy, I am paying him to do the job. And he never disappoints me—the job always gets done. Nothing else really matters to me. It's a deal that we both understand and live by.

People in my business are always telling me how much they want an employee like Vic. I tell them they would never be able to have an employee like Vic. First, they wouldn't trust their Vic to really run the business. They are too protective and territorial and think that they must be personally involved in every detail of the business. Second, they wouldn't pay him enough to make a good living. People want great employees and yet want to pay them just enough money to eke by and won't trust them enough to do the job they were hired to do. Yeah, that philosophy will get you quality people every time!

Your argument to my Vic story is probably something like "Not everyone works in a small office like yours, Larry. We work in a big company and it matters that people actually be there. Neat idea, but it won't work for everyone." Good argument. And you are absolutely right. Scope up from the details of my example and look at the principles involved. *Reward results. Empower people to get results. Appreciate results. Judge results.* Results are everything. This is the real message to those who do the work and those who manage the work: Work is getting the desired result.

So how are you doing?

Are you an employee who believes that appearing busy is the key to success? Or are you one of those stupid managers who like to see people being busy? Wait, did I just say that a manager who likes to see people being busy is stupid? Yes, that's what I said. If you like watching busy people instead of productive people, you are stupid. Some people can look so busy, you actually think they are getting things done. Be careful. Look at the results.

Remember, you are paid for results, and you are paying for results. Results indicate how productive a person is and have little to do with how busy a person is.

There is nothing sadder than to find out an employee is excellent at doing something that doesn't need to be done at all.

"Never mistake activity for achievement."

—JOHN WOODEN, legendary UCLA basketball coach

"The really idle man gets nowhere. The perpetually busy man does not get much further." —SIR WILLIAM HENEAGE OGILVIE

Pay people well

Pay people well when they deliver the results. Remember this: You can't get rich keeping other people broke. Share the wealth.

It is amazing how some companies brag about how they can get their work done so cheaply. Tell me, did you ever get the best work done for you by the lowest bidder? Probably not. You do get what you pay for. So pay as much as you can and a little more. If you become known as a person who pays well, you will attract better employees to work for you. And well-paid employees aren't always looking for a better job for a nickel more at every opportunity. You build loyalty when you pay people well.

"If you pay peanuts, you get monkeys." —SIR JAMES GOLDSMITH

How money and service are tied together

Service is the key to each aspect of business success. The better you serve your customer, the better the customer will in turn serve you. Service is the key to selling. When you sell customers a product that makes their lives easier, more efficient, or more fun, you have served them well. Leadership is about serving the people who work for you. Each area of business is defined by the service it provides. The better you get at providing that service, the more valuable you will be to your organization. The more valuable you are, the more you will be paid.

People who make $6.00 an hour are paid that because they provide $6.00 worth of service and it takes them an hour to do it. Face it: "Do you want fries with that?" isn't brain surgery. People who make $25,000 an hour are paid that because they provide $25,000 worth of service and it takes them an hour to do it. Face it: That *is* brain surgery.

The difference is not the hour. For both individuals it was the same sixty minutes. The difference is the service provided within the hour. The key is to put more service into the hour. Most people spend their energy figuring out how to put more hours in the service.

Something most people have forgotten: you have a boss

Everyone has one. Regardless of how big the company is or how small it is, everyone answers to someone. Even the "big boss" has a boss. That boss is called the stockholder(s). Everyone works for someone. Even if you are the sole owner of your company, you have a boss. There is simply no such thing as self-employed.

Your boss has the right to direct your activities. That's why she is the boss. She gets to tell you what to do. She gets to tell you when to come to work and when to go home. She can tell you what to work on, when to take a break, who to work with, and when to go on vacation. The boss determines what you do, when you do it, and how much you get paid to do it. If you don't do your job the way the boss wants it done, then she has every right to point that out to you and complain. That is her job. If she doesn't do her job, then *her* boss will point that out to her, and she will have to deal with the consequences of not doing her job. Get it?

The ultimate boss, however, is the customer. We all have customers, though we call them by different names. Attorneys call them the clients. Doctors call them the patients. Authors call them the readers. Speakers call them the audience. Most businesses just call them the customer. It doesn't matter what you call them; we must all understand that the customer is the ultimate boss. Customers have the money, and you are there to serve them in order to get them to share that money with you and your company. They decide whether you will survive and how much money you make. The customer also gets to tell you when to come to work and when to go home. And if you don't do your job correctly, they have the right to point that out and complain. Customers are the ultimate boss, and they matter more than any other entity in business.

I have plenty to say about serving the customer, and will in a few chapters. I just want you to understand that the boss has rights. You work for a boss—probably many of them—and they pay you for results. Don't complicate it more than that.

A personal rant

We don't live in a perfect world. If we did, seniority wouldn't matter, unions wouldn't exist, and everyone would get hired, fired, paid, and promoted solely on their performance. The person who contributes most to the bottom line, treats people with respect, works hard, works smart, and serves customers well would be the employee who is most rewarded.

But that isn't going to happen . . . yet. Not until we take back our businesses from the control of the government and the control of the labor unions. Not until companies get some backbone and managers, leaders, and workers start doing what is right without the worry of lawsuits. Not until customers get the guts to demand good service and not settle for anything less. Not until manufacturers make products they are willing to stand behind. Not until businesses quit looking for loopholes to get out of their warranties and guarantees and start looking for ways to do more than provide only minimal service. Until then, we just have to do the best we can with what we have.

Whew! I feel much better.

Larry's short list for getting results:

- *Focus on results. Results are everything and they never lie.*
- *Explain the big picture to all employees so they know why they are doing their jobs.*
- *Whatever you have or are experiencing is what makes up your results.*
- *Put more service into every hour, not more hours into the service.*
- *The number-one reason why results aren't what they should be: apathy.*
- *Well-paid employees are typically loyal employees.*
- *You are not paid for effort; you are paid for results.*

CHAPTER 5

"Your results are your own damn fault"

That hurts, doesn't it? I just told you that your results are your own damn fault. So dump the excuses. It's not your stupid boss's fault. It isn't the fault of your asinine coworkers. Stop blaming your spouse, your brother-in-law, your kids, your first-grade teacher, the fact that you aren't sleeping well or that you are getting older or that you have male-pattern baldness. Affirmative action, the union, tenure, or office politics won't work either. None of it flies. The only thing you need to know is this: Your results are *your* fault and no one else's. How much money you have, how happy you are, the quality of your relationships, where you live, the car you drive—you name it, it's all your fault.

Don't agree with me? It doesn't really matter. You see, I don't make the rules. I have just learned to play by them. Your life is your fault. You created it. You made it just the way it is.

Your thoughts, your words, and your actions caused it. It's your fault. Deal with it.

If your life sucks, it's because YOU suck.

Too harsh? Too bad. This is not a hold-your-hand book. I am not going to play footsies with you. If you want that, go read one of those cute little parable business books.

Let me take my philosophy of personal responsibility to a business level:

*If your business sucks, it is because
as a businessperson, you suck.*

If your sales suck, it's because as a salesperson, you suck.

If your employees suck, it's because as a manager, you suck.

*If your customer service sucks, it's because you
deliver sucky customer service!*

Hopefully you laughed at that little rant. If you didn't, it might have been a little too close to the truth for you and it made you want to scream something like:

"Whoa, that's not fair!"

What makes you think life is fair? It isn't. But this isn't about fair or unfair, it's about the truth. And while the truth doesn't always seem fair, it is still the truth. If a person does stupid things, he will get stupid results. If a person does intelligent things, then his results will reflect that. When a business does stupid things, the business will get stupid results. When a business does smart things, then the results will reflect it.

Besides, it's a simple fix. It will require some hard work, but I promise it won't be complicated. I am going to give you simple, direct instructions on how you can rise from the depths of "suckitude" to the pinnacle of success. You will sell more, manage better, serve your customers more effectively, make decisions quickly, and discover all it takes to be happier, more successful, and more prosperous. I promise I am about to give you practical, usable ideas that are easy to implement and will give you fast results. That's my deal with you. But none of those ideas will matter one iota if you don't buy into this one simple concept:

It's your own damn fault. Always and without exception. If you will meet me at this beginning point and accept it, then you will have the key to opening the door to personal and business success.

That is going to be your biggest challenge. We would rather do anything than accept that our results are our own fault. Individuals don't want to admit it, and businesses are just as unwilling.

Businesses love to blame others for not doing well. They blame the government, the economy, upsizing, downsizing, rightsizing, technology, stupid management, stupid employees, foreign competition, Wal-Mart and the other "big box" stores, unions, affirmative action, OSHA, the ACLU, taxes, outsourcing, the Internet, high prices, the law and lawyers, interest rates, banks, and on and on and on.

Whining runs rampant throughout the world of business: from the minimum-wage fast-food employee who complains about the fact that his boss is on his ass to wash his hands more, to the CEO who gripes about the feds and how interest rates are ruining his business.

To stop the excuses and deal with your situation like a responsible person, try this:

The mirror principle

If you don't like things the way they are, there is only one place to go to lay blame: the mirror.

Do this quick exercise: Go to a mirror. Really, get off your butt right this minute, take the book with you, and head toward a mirror. The bathroom is always a good place to get honest with yourself, so go to the bathroom. Go ahead—I'm waiting! Now gaze into the mirror, look yourself in the eye, and say the following:

"This is all my fault. I created this mess. I caused it through my thoughts, my words, and my actions. Only I can fix it. It's up to me."

Okay, now you have just been honest. (Even though I doubt you actually went to the bathroom and stood in front of the mirror.)

An alarming bit of reality

You like it just the way it is. You like your results. Even if your results suck, you like them.

"No, I don't. I want more than this. I hate not doing well."

Bull. You are perfectly happy with the way things are, or you would have done something about it. You haven't fixed the problem, you have only complained about the problem. You must be happier with the problem than you would be with the solution, because you are spending more time talking about the problem than you are working on the solution. And you can't do both at the same time.

If you aren't actively fixing your problems, you like them. Or at least you don't hate them enough to do anything about them.

Larry's short list for doing better:

- *Stop complaining about your results. (No one really cares, anyway.)*
- *Whining about the problem only prolongs the problem.*
- *Take a realistic look at your results and think about what you have done or not done in the past that contributed to them.*
- *Go to the closest mirror, look yourself in the eye, and say, "This is all my fault." Take responsibility.*
- *Do a reality check and admit that change has been going on for a good long while and you survived. You will survive this, too.*
- *Make a list of what you are going to do differently in the future to change your results.*
- *Doing better is the result of deciding to do better and then taking action on that decision. Get busy!*

CHAPTER 6

You don't have to love your job (*but it helps*)

It is a solid business principle that people who enjoy what they do are better at what they do. People who do not enjoy what they do are just never going to be as good at their jobs as people who love their jobs. That is just the way it is. Excellence ultimately comes from enjoyment. This is a fact—maybe.

In my speeches to my corporate audiences, I use the line "When it quits being fun—quit!" When meeting planners watch my DVD while considering me for a speaking engagement, they sometimes call my manager to tell him, "We have decided to hire Larry, but there is one line in his speech we just don't want him to use. It's the line where he says, 'When it quits being fun—quit.' Because if he shows up and says that, they will *all* quit."

I once did a speech for eleven people: the company president and ten vice-presidents. I used the line "When it quits being fun—quit" and then paused to take a quick drink of water. One of the vice-presidents interrupted and said, "Just a minute, Larry . . . I quit." Then he got up, picked up his stuff, and left the room. Trust me; that will put a damper on a seminar in a hurry! The president of the company immediately suggested we take a break. You think? When he came back after about twenty minutes he asked that I not say anything like that again. Now, that's a funny story—but it's also just sad. Sad because the guy had pushed himself to the point where it would take something like that for him to get the nerve to face his unhappiness. I later got a nice letter from him saying how thankful he was that he had finally been given permission to just be happy. He also said that he had found a job for more money and was having more fun than he had ever imagined. If you are like him and need permission to be happy, then please let me give it to you now. Go forth and be happy! If that means you need to quit your job—quit. But don't quit without something else lined up. No reason to be stupid about it!

Love what you do. Chances are when you first got your job you were thrilled with it. You loved your office, your desk, your chair, your cash register, your workstation, or your cubicle. But now it's old and familiar and you hate it. Or do you? Maybe you just got stuck in a rut. That can be fixed.

You and your job have a relationship

Just like a relationship with a person can become stale, so can your relationship with your job. When your marriage becomes a little boring, what you should do is spice it up a bit. You should go back to the stuff that brought you together to begin with. You should remind yourself what made you fall in love with that person. Maybe you need to make yourself a list of what attracted you in the first place. When you have done that, then you need to take action. You might want to start having regular dates again like you did when you first started going out. You may want a new wardrobe, so you can dress up again for your husband. You need to clean up a bit before you traipse off to the bedroom. You need to make yourself more attractive to your partner. Guys, you need to hit the gym so you can drop a pound or twenty for your wife. While it may be hard at first, anything worth having is worth working to keep. So give it some effort. This is solid advice for any relationship.

It is also solid advice for your job. Your relationship with your job may need to be spiced up a bit. Here's a suggestion for you: Make a list of what you originally loved about your job. Write down everything. Keep it simple. I mean idiot simple. Things like your chair. Your uniform. The window in your office. The color of the carpet. Your coworkers. Your parking place. The subway ride. The coffee room. I don't know what it might be, and I don't really care what it is. It's not my list, it's yours. You know what you liked about your job when you first got it, so write it down. Do it to remind yourself of the good old days—days you might want to recapture. Re-sell yourself on why this is a good job that you enjoy doing. Then take action on the list and on yourself. Dress up a bit more for your job just like you would for your spouse if you were trying to rekindle the flame. Lose some of the fat that has accumulated over the years. Clean up your office—throw away some things in order to get a fresh start with your job and your space. This is easy stuff. There's no brain surgery here. You know what I'm going for. You can do it.

When you love your job, enjoy your job, and have fun at your job, you will be better at your job.

The big but

And it's a big fat "but." Sometimes you will not enjoy or love your work. Regardless of how much you try or what steps you go through, you just won't be able to get that love or enjoyment back. Sometimes it will suck and you will hate it. That's when you remember why you do it—you duck your head and just keep going until you can enjoy it again some other day. Besides, you made a deal when you took the position to do the job even when you didn't feel like it and weren't having a good day. Your coworkers, customers, and the company shouldn't have to suffer just because today you aren't having fun at what you do.

The lies about business success and the lying liars who tell them

Business writers and speakers will lie to you and say that the key to business success is to love your job. Wait! I just told you that too. Then I am also a liar. Yes, I admit it. While loving your job is one of the keys to being successful at your job, it isn't absolutely necessary. You don't have to love your job in order to be excellent at it. *But it helps.*

Passion. The motivational bozos all say that you have to be passionate about your job. Passion is way overrated. Sales trainers love telling salespeople that if they are passionate about their product, they can sell it. In the business of professional speaking, you hear all the time that you have to be passionate about your subject. All a big lie! You don't have to be passionate to be successful in your job or to be good at your job. *But it helps.*

Enthusiasm. Sure, that's the key to success. No, that isn't it either. *But it helps.*

Enjoy your job. If you have fun doing it, you will be successful. I have said this in my speeches for years. "Excellence comes from enjoyment." I even started this chapter with that line. I even take it further: People who enjoy their jobs are better at their jobs and people who do not enjoy their jobs are probably never going to be any good at their jobs. Isn't that good stuff? Sure it is, I said it! But . . . and it's another of those big fat buts again, it isn't exactly true. You don't have to enjoy your job to be great at it. *But it helps.*

Bottom line: It takes more than passion. It takes more than enthusiasm. It takes more than love and enjoyment.

My friend Joe Calloway, author of *Becoming a Category of One* and *Indispensable*, and about the best business speaker I have ever heard, has for years said that he is not passionate about his job. He enjoys it, but he certainly isn't passionate about it. He is passionate about his wife, his daughter, his friends, and his family. He speaks and writes about customer service and branding. As he puts it, "How can you be passionate about customer service and branding?" Good question. Beats me; I'm certainly not. Yet Joe is the best I know at what he does. He is also just about the most successful guy I know in the speaking and consulting business. Why? It certainly isn't passion and love and fun and enjoyment. It's because he is just so damn good at it. In fact, when I told him I was writing this paragraph about him, he wrote me back and said, "Just because you are following your bliss, it doesn't mean anybody's going to pay you for it." I love that line. They pay you because you are good at what you do and because you serve them well. You don't have to be passionate. *But it helps.*

Love it, but love it enough

If you tell me you love your job and you aren't great at your job, I'll call you a liar. That's right—a liar. If you really love your job, you will do what it takes to be good at your job. That's what love does to you. It causes you to become better. When you love someone, you work on yourself so you will be a better person for her. When you love your job, you will work on yourself so you will be better for your job. You will love it enough to be good at it. If you aren't doing that, you don't love your job at all; you love going to that place where you hang out and they pay you for it.

The real key to success on the job is to be good at what you do. Those other things help. They help a lot. They are definitely a huge factor in overall success and you won't catch me saying they aren't. But they aren't the key. The real key to business success is to be good at what you do. Excellence does not come just from enjoyment or passion or love or fun. Excellence comes from study. Excellence comes from experience. It comes from screwing up and doing it wrong until you finally, *finally*, **finally** get it right. And it comes from good old-fashioned hard work! The other things help, but alone they are mostly hot air. Sweat changes things—not hot air.

Once more, only this time uglier:

The next time you hear yourself saying, "I don't like my job," remember this: No one cares. You aren't paid to *like* your job. You are paid to *do* your job.

You actually do your job only 10 percent of the time

I'm not talking about how much you work. I am talking about how much of your time is actually spent doing your job.

I am a professional speaker more than two hundred days per year. Yet, I spend less than one hundred hours per year on stage speaking. The rest of my time as a speaker is spent traveling to and from the speech; waiting to speak; messing with hotels, room service, airlines, cabs, rental cars, and all of the other things that go into my job. How much of my time being a professional speaker is spent speaking? Not too much.

What about you? Perhaps you are a salesperson. How much time do you spend actually selling? My guess is about 10 percent. The rest of the time is spent doing all the non-selling stuff associated with your job.

Doctor? I bet that only about 10 percent of your time is spent with patients, practicing medicine. The rest is spent doing all of the other stuff that is necessary to maintain a profitable medical practice, but it isn't spent "doctoring."

See what I mean? Fall in love with the 10 percent of your job that is really your job and just put up with the rest of it—the other 90 percent—because it's just part of what must be done to get you to the 10 percent that you enjoy.

Larry's short list for loving your job:

- *Love and enjoy what you do enough to be amazing at it.*
- *It takes more than passion, enthusiasm, love, and enjoyment to be great at your job; you must be good at what you do.*
- *You aren't paid to like your job; you are paid to do your job.*
- *Some days you must put up with 90 percent of your job to get to the 10 percent you really enjoy.*
- *Spice up your job a little to rekindle the passion you once had for it.*

CHAPTER 7

Become invaluable

Carolynn, my shipping queen

I do all of my shipping and receiving at my area UPS Store. I also use that as my personal address, since I travel a lot and I don't want things stacking up at my house, nor do I want people to know where I live. (I've got to protect myself from all of the people who don't like what I have to say!) I know all of the folks at the UPS Store. I am a loud guy who admittedly has some quirks and who is easily recognizable. I also get a lot of cool stuff that they are always curious about. Trust me, when you ask someone to sign for the skull of a water buffalo, you get his attention. Carolynn is my main person at the store. I rely on her completely. She takes care of my stuff, always has a smile for me, and gives me a feeling of confidence when I hand over something important that simply has to get where it's going when it is supposed to. The other people who work there are all great, but my connection is with Carolynn. She has read my books, watched my DVDs, and listened to my CDs. She even has a Larry bobblehead next to her computer. She "gets" me and what I do. Even when I moved to a different house and this UPS Store was no longer the closest, I made the decision that I wouldn't change, because I didn't want to give up Carolynn and have to "train" someone to deal with me all over again. She even gives me a dark chocolate Hershey's Kiss sometimes, and that makes me a very dedicated customer!

I noticed a Help Wanted sign one day as I entered the store. When I asked if they were just hiring more people or whether someone was leaving, Carolynn told me that she was the one leaving. I dropped to the floor and sobbed. Not really, but I was disappointed. I had grown to count on her over my five-year stint with her store. We were buddies; she watched out for me and my stuff, and now she was leaving. I told my wife I didn't know if I could keep going there. I told her we might have to change locations for the one closer to our house. My confidence in the whole organization was shaken because Carolynn was leaving. I just wasn't sure that the new people were going to be able to handle things.

Time has passed. Were the new people able to handle my things and give me good service? Of course they were. Not like Carolynn, but still good, competent service. The lesson is that I counted on Carolynn so much I didn't even think of it as the UPS Store, I thought of it as the place I took things so that Carolynn could take care of them. I trusted her, the individual, not the organization. Through her efforts to get to know me, take care of my stuff, and build my trust in her, she became invaluable to me.

When your customers count on you more than your organization, then you have become invaluable.

"Okay, but how do I do it?"

Work hard on your job— and harder on yourself

What are you doing on your own time to become better at what you do? Are you reading books? Watching videos of successful people? Are you studying your products or your competitors? Most would say, "Hell, no! My time is *my* time. If they want me to do that stuff, they should pay me to do it."

If you adhere to this popular belief, then you are doomed. Even if you bust your butt on the job, you don't understand the big picture of what it takes to be successful. You may be the world's greatest salesclerk, giving it all you've got every day, but if all you do is work hard while you are at work, then all you are ever going to be is the world's greatest hard-working salesclerk.

Your future is up to you, not your employer. You have to get better in order for your circumstances to get better, and that must be done on your own time. Some employers do offer educational programs for their employees, and it is amazing how few take advantage of them. I guess they are just too busy to learn.

Improve yourself in any way you can, every time you have a chance. It doesn't take much time to read a great book on success. About thirty minutes before bed will do it. Thirty minutes that would make you more attractive to your employer and might move you up the chain a bit when it comes to promotion time. Or when it comes time to lay people off.

People get fired, demoted, passed over for promotion, not given the raise, or denied privileges for one reason more than any other reason: They just didn't have the results to deserve anything better. You may not have been told that is the reason you didn't get promoted. Very few managers are really honest enough to tell the truth to their employees. What they say is usually couched in much more soothing terms than "Your results suck—you deserve this." But regardless of the reason given, the prevailing truth will always be the fact that you just didn't produce results worthy of keeping you around. Someone else did. Bet that ticks you off, doesn't it? You thought you got fired because the company was downsizing. You thought the other guy got promoted because he was a big kiss-up. You may have convinced yourself that you didn't get the raise because people at your job just aren't fair. But the truth is, you didn't work hard enough. You didn't get the things done that needed to be done.

If you want to make sure you are in line for every good thing your company has to offer, then become invaluable. Be the smartest person in the company about the products and services your company offers. Know more about the competition and the marketplace than anyone else. Get there first and leave last. Do the stuff no one else wants to do. Work fast. Learn to make decisions quickly. Take personal responsibility. Never whine. Become known as a person who gets things done. Do more than is expected of you. Get the results. In other words: Work!

This is job security at its finest. Just become the employee that your company can't live without. Become the person that your customers can't live without. Become the person your company, your boss, your coworkers, and your customers count on, need, and want to have around.

Don't complicate this idea. Something very simple can be the key to you becoming invaluable. I love Boston. The city is beautiful and full of history, and has some of the best food in the country. I get there two or three times a year and always end up at the same seafood restaurant. I'm almost always alone, so I just sit at the bar. One of the bartenders and I usually chat for a minute or two as he takes my order, which is always the same: chowder (pronounced "chowdah" when in Boston) and crab cakes. The first time I went there, Hugh the bartender asked my name and what I did for a living. From that point on, he has never forgotten it. When I hit the door, he calls out my name and asks if I want my usual. I asked him one day how he could remember not only my name but exactly what I drank and what I ordered to eat when I was in there only a couple of times a year. He said he made up his mind when he went to work there that he would remember people's names and something about them. I told him I was impressed beyond words. He laughed and said, "Yeah, I think the main reason they keep me around is because I know everyone who walks through the door and what they eat and drink. People love to be called by name—and they tip better too!" From personal experience, I know they do indeed. I am certain I could find better chowder and crab cakes at fifty other restaurants in Boston, but Hugh wouldn't be there, so I'll just keep going to the same place and getting my usual. And I'll be tipping way more than necessary because of it.

Is what Hugh did all that hard? Yes, it's hard to learn people's names and their usual order. But is it complicated? No. Hugh is invaluable to that restaurant, and now to me as a customer. Plus, he makes more money because of it. A little extra effort and everyone wins.

Who are you?

I was recently giving a speech to an organization of two hundred people. When I got there, about twenty people in the production company introduced themselves to me, told me their titles, and said they were at my disposal to help me in any way I needed. I immediately knew I was in trouble, because this meeting was totally overproduced. You just don't need twenty people to put together a meeting for only two hundred people. When I speak at a meeting, I need a table onstage for my props and one at the back of the room to sign my books. Everyone involved in this meeting knew in advance that I needed both of those tables. Yet, when I got there, they weren't in place. I told everyone who introduced themselves to me that my tables weren't there and I needed to get them set up. I told the meeting planner, the production manager, the sound guy, the stage manager, you name it, I told everyone I could find and was assured each time it would be taken care of. I was finally close to running out of time and needed to set up my props and my product table before the break was over and the attendees came back into the room. A production company guy suddenly appeared and said, "You don't look happy; what do you need?" I told him I needed two tables and showed him where I needed them. He said not to worry; he would take care of it right then. He immediately set up my tables, and as I thanked him, I asked him what *his* title was, since everyone else had been so quick to tell me theirs. He said, "I'm just the guy who gets shit done." That is what we all really want: just a guy who gets shit done. Become known as that person.

Most people, however, are like the other people on this crew who were trying to impress me with their titles and promising all they would do for me, but when called upon to actually do it, they were totally ineffective. Lip service instead of customer service.

You run into both types of people every day. Most could easily be done without—they bring nothing to the table. Then you find that one invaluable gem of a person, a guy who just gets things done.

Very few people focus on becoming invaluable. In fact, most people spend their time on the job becoming anything but invaluable. They do exactly the opposite of what they should be doing.

They don't get results. They don't have a clue about their product line. They don't understand the industry they work in. They don't know their competition. They don't make any effort to get along with their coworkers. They act as if their company owes them a living. They call in sick when they aren't. They complain all the time. They don't read. They don't study. They don't listen. Many don't even know their hours of operation. Most can't even give you directions to get to their business. They consider the customer an imposition. They work just hard enough so they won't get fired. They are leeches—sucking the life, the money, and the value out of their company.

I-N-T

Today, Not Tomorrow.

This should be the motto of every employee, every manager, every leader, and every business.

If it's a good idea, do it today. Not tomorrow. A good idea rarely gets better over time.

"A good idea implemented today is better than a perfect idea implemented tomorrow." —GEN. GEORGE S. PATTON

If you are one of those people who just are never in a hurry—one of those who say, "There is plenty of time," "What's the rush?" "Don't worry, we've got all the time in the world," or anything similar to any of those statements—I'll do my best to be as polite and delicate as I possibly can be as I say this about you: You are an idiot. Are we clear? There is NO time. There is always a rush. You don't have all the time in the world. Hurry up!

When should you call the customer? Today.

When should you praise the employee who did a great job? Today.

When should you thank a coworker for helping you on that project? Today.

When should you fire that incompetent employee? Today.

When should you clean your desk? Today.

When should you do anything worth doing? Today.

Not tomorrow. Never tomorrow. Always today.

"You cannot escape the responsibility of tomorrow by evading it

today." —ABRAHAM LINCOLN

Speed keeps you on track

When you work fast, you also have a tendency to do the right thing. I believe when you think too much about what should be done, your mind starts to scheme and try to come up with shortcuts. You start to think about the easy thing to do instead of the *right* thing to do. The right thing to do usually comes straight from your gut. When you work fast, you tend to work more from the gut, because your mind simply doesn't have as much time to justify an easier way to do things.

Am I against thinking about things? Am I saying just jump in without giving things much thought? Not at all. I am just making the case for creating a sense of urgency.

I believe that work should be done when it can be done, and it can almost always be done now. Few things ever need to be put off. Doing something now usually means that you are working more from instinct. I believe people have good instincts. I believe people will usually do the right thing when they need to, if it is expected of them. When you expect the work to get done quickly and when you reward work that is done quickly, the work will get done quickly. On the other hand, when people have lots of time to plan and think and scheme, their minds start to wander and they start to look for ways to cut corners.

When you expect the work to get done quickly

and when you reward work that is done quickly,

the work will get done quickly.

It's kind of like kids in high school who come up with elaborate plans to cheat on a test. In most cases, they would actually get better results in much less time if they would just learn the material. Instead, they spend more time than it would have taken to learn coming up with ways not to learn.

The downside to becoming invaluable

"What? There's a downside?"

Sadly, there is.

Coworkers will make fun of you, talk behind your back, criticize you, call you a kiss-ass and a company man. Some may even say bad things about your mama. So what? You work to feed *your* family, not theirs, so screw them!

Even your so-called friends will talk about you. I learned a long time ago, as I became more and more successful, that while your friends want you to be successful, they don't want you to be more successful than they are.

That's why it isn't always smart to get really close to people you work with. You only work with them. You should respect them and enjoy the camaraderie, but you don't need to or have to share your dreams and aspirations with them.

I have found it best to live by this credo: What you think of me is none of my business.

Bad things happen to good employees

I am not oblivious to what is going on in business today. I know the economy can go in the toilet and some companies, simply because of the type of business they are involved in, will be forced to lay off good, hard-working men and women. It happens. I'm sorry.

No one is bulletproof.

If something bad does happen to you, my advice is to suck it up, don't whine or complain about it, get off your butt and go get another job. When you get the new job, just start over and become invaluable at that business.

And please don't tell me you can't get another job. There are plenty of jobs out there. Just maybe not doing what you were doing before. Okay, you were an engineer making $90,000 a year for a huge manufacturing company. But now your unemployment checks have run out and your insurance is going away and things are looking bad for your family. You are falling behind on your payments and you wonder what you are going to do next month. You have sent your resume to other employers in the area trying to get another job as an engineer—something commensurate with your skills and past accomplishments. But it just isn't happening for you. So what are you going to do? Here's an idea: Get a job. Stop looking for a career. You have bills to pay. Take a job. Any job. Get something where you have to say, "You want me to supersize that?" It doesn't matter what job you get to pay your bills. Just get employed. It will do you good. The best time to find a job is when you already have one.

"But I'm better than that! Do you know who I am?"

Yeah, I know who you are: You are the person with no job and no money. And no, you are not better than that. Don't be stupid and let your ego tell you that you are too good for something. You aren't. You aren't too good to work at anything that puts food on the table and money in the bank, and takes care of your family. It may not be a job you are particularly proud of or plan on doing for long, but you are not too good to do it. You have commitments. Take care of them.

Recently while shooting an episode of my A&E television show, *Big Spender*, I worked with a man who had been laid off from his job six months earlier. The company experienced a severe economic setback and was forced to let people go. He was making $50,000 a year and had been employed with his company for fourteen years. For six months he had been making excuses about not getting a regular job for $12 an hour because he used to be worth $50,000. I told him that I used to have hair too. I explained that what he used to make after working for a company for fourteen years had little bearing on what he was worth to another company in a different industry. Besides, $12 an hour was $12 more than he made for all those hours he had been unemployed over the past six months.

On another episode, I told a woman who had almost no money and was living with her dad (who was working two jobs to take care of her, her two sons, and her boyfriend) that she needed to get a job. I suggested that she take anything she could find to start bringing in some income and to make her feel better about herself. I firmly believe that we all like ourselves better when we are contributing. She said that she had worked at jobs that she didn't like in the past and now she wanted a career that she could enjoy every single day, so there was no way she was going to take a job just to make money. Here she is, broke and living off someone else and won't take a job because she might not like it all the time. She said she was better than that. I was appalled. There is no way you will enjoy your job every minute of the day. I'd love to get paid just to sit on my patio and watch the sun go down while drinking a scotch, smoking a great cigar, and petting my two bulldogs. But I figured out a long time ago it wasn't going to happen, so instead I pack a bag, catch a plane, take a taxi ride, stay in a hotel, then yell at people for an hour or so and do it all over again. It's what they pay me for. I don't love it every minute. But I try not to complain about it too much.

I recently got into a cab at the airport in Washington, D.C. Soon after we began our journey, we were stuck in a traffic jam.

This infuriated the driver and he started screaming and yelling about how he was better than this. I tried to ignore him, but I have a problem ignoring stupidity on any level. He went on to say he was not even a cabdriver; he was a highly skilled, highly trained mechanical engineer. With no prompting from me, he went on to say that the company where he had been working for nearly fifteen years had laid him off when it ran into some financial problems. He just wouldn't shut up about all of it. Life was unfair, his former employers were idiots, he was better than this, he deserved better, and on and on and on. I finally told him that this was a sad story but that for today, at least for the next thirty minutes or so, he was not an engineer. He used to be an engineer, but at least for today, he was a cabdriver and I would appreciate him just driving the cab, doing the best job he could as a cabdriver. I told him bad things happen to people all the time, but complaining never fixed anything, and I was tired of listening to him complain. I didn't do it to him and I didn't want to hear about it. It worked. He shut up for the rest of my ride. The next guy in his cab probably heard about what a jerk I was, but at least I didn't have to listen to him whine.

He was making a fatal mistake in some ways, yet doing the right thing in other ways. He was doing the right thing because he took a job to pay his bills. He was doing the wrong thing because he was letting his ego dictate his happiness.

You won't always have the job you want. You won't always get the employment that deserves your talents. Tough. You are employed. Many aren't. Give thanks. Work hard. Do what you are paid to do and look for something better while you're at it.

Larry's short list for becoming invaluable:

- *Know everything you can about your company and its product line, and about how business is conducted.*
- *Stay out of personal conflicts with coworkers and customers and rise above pettiness.*
- *Put the customer first when making decisions.*
- *Understand your competition.*
- *Pursue excellence in every area of your activities.*
- *Work fast.*

CHAPTER 8

The holy of holies

Would you walk into St. Patrick's Cathedral and cuss, tell filthy jokes, spit on the floor, or be profane in any way? No. Even if you were an atheist, you wouldn't do it. You would respect the building and the people in it enough to know better. We should be the same way about our places of business. The building should be a place where we respect the work that goes on there, the purpose of the organization, the people who earn a living there in order to take care of their families, and the customers who share their money to keep us in business and employed. In most businesses this respect has been lost. Customers are seen as an imposition, coworkers are made fun of or criticized, and we regularly trash the competition. This has to stop. We have to rebuild the organization from the ground up based on the principle of respect.

This should be the credo of every business:

This is a sacred place
where we only speak well of ourselves,

we only speak well of our organization,
we only speak well of our competitors,
and we only speak well of our customers.

Speak well of each other

I recently went with my son to buy a new plasma television. We shopped around and finally found a great television at a great price at Best Buy. When we told the clerk we wanted to buy it, he said he would have to check to see if they had any in stock. They didn't. I asked if any of the other Best Buy stores in the area had any in stock. He said he would go check his computer to find out. When he came back, he told us that another store about fifteen miles away had one according to the computer, but the computer was often wrong. I asked him if he could check with them. He rolled his eyes and wandered off. In a few minutes, he came back with a scrap of paper with a phone number written on it; he said that was the number and we could call them ourselves if we wanted. I asked him why he didn't do it himself, since that would seem more like his job than mine. He said he didn't have the time. I looked around the store and commented that it was a Tuesday afternoon and I could count nine clerks standing around talking to one another, so it didn't seem like he was too busy to help a customer spend nearly four thousand dollars. He replied that the real problem was that sometimes you had to wait a really long time for the people at the other store to answer, because they were slow and it took them forever to answer their phone or get you an answer about their inventory. I said, "In other words, they don't really care about helping the customer either, right?" He rolled his eyes once again (this was the only thing the guy was really good at, I believe), wandered off without a word, and came back with someone even less interested in helping us. He said that this guy would call the other store. The result? The computer was indeed wrong and the other store didn't have the television in stock either. The television would have to be ordered, and it would take three days to get it.

The synopsis: This was an indifferent employee who didn't care about the customer, his store, his company, or its profits and he had happily badmouthed another store and its employees.

Your coworkers will mess up and you will know it. But it is not up to you to point that out to the customer. You represent your coworkers and should speak well of them in front of the customer even when they have been idiots and screwed things up.

It is no one's business what you think of your coworkers, so keep it to yourself. It is certainly not the customer's business what you think. The only thing the customers need to know is that you care about and appreciate their business. Everything else is irrelevant.

We ultimately made some calls to other Best Buy stores and located the television ourselves and received both the excellent price and excellent service.

Speak well of the customer

I was checking in at the front desk of a hotel in Orlando when another clerk at the front desk took a call from a man trying to find the hotel. Obviously this was someone from out of town, since people who stay at hotels in the town in which they live are usually philanderers having clandestine meetings of the illicit type. From the half of the conversation I could hear, the man was pretty close but just couldn't seem to find his way through the city streets to get to the hotel. The clerk was becoming very frustrated with him, and she just kept saying, "What's around you? I don't know that place, what else is around you?" Finally she screamed at the man, "I don't know north and south, I only know right and left—hang on." She then put the poor guy on hold and told her coworker, who was helping me at the time, that this guy was an idiot and he could just sit on hold for a while. She then stood there tapping her foot, letting the guy wait. I asked her why he was the one who was the idiot; he at least knew north and south, which obviously made him a lot smarter than she. I also asked her if she realized he was coming to her hotel to pay money for a room that would eventually work around to paying her salary. She looked at me and said, "Oh, brother!" and went into the back room. I told her coworker who was helping me check in that I wanted her name so I could report her to the manager, and she said, "I am the manager." I then suggested she fire the clerk for her rudeness and the fact that during all of this, the customer was still on hold. Her reply to me was "Hey, it's hard to find good people." I said, "I bet that's what your manager says about you, too." She didn't appreciate my comments. (Why do I run into that so much?)

Why did I have to hear that exchange between an employee and a customer? Why did the clerk treat the customer that way? Why did the manager not seem to care? They know there are no consequences for behaving rudely. And they see no correlation between what they do and what they get paid.

Is all of this pretty typical? Sadly, yes. Remember what I said earlier about apathy being such a big problem?

Speak well of the competition

Yes, even the competition. Never build yourself up by tearing another down. Don't think that talking bad about your competition makes customers want to spend their money with you. Refuse to let anyone in your organization speak ill of the competition—especially in front of a customer.

In fact, I love it when a company openly praises their competition. It makes me think more of both companies. Nothing builds confidence in a company and its abilities more than when they say to me, "That's not really what we are best at; we could do it, but you really should call XYZ Company for that." I'll do my best to spend money with both when that happens. My bet is that you will too.

"Do not hold the delusion that your advancement is accomplished by crushing others." —Marcus Tullius Cicero

Respect the space

Look around your place of business. Are there weeds growing up between the cracks of the sidewalk in front of your building? Is the parking lot littered? Whether you like it or not, that will have an effect on what people think about the quality of your product and your service. Not fair? I don't have to be fair—I'm the customer.

Is the carpet stained? You don't have trustworthy people working there. Not fair? Too bad: It's what I think.

Cigarette butts by the front door? You don't care about my business enough to sweep your entry. I'll go elsewhere. Not fair? I don't have to be fair. Besides, you'll never know about it. I'll just go away and spend my money with someone else who bothers sweeping the entrance.

Dirty uniforms on your waiters? Your food is tainted and I will get ptomaine. Not fair? Too bad: I believe it, so it's true.

Stupidity factoid: We care about our customers. Just not enough to keep the restrooms clean.

The little stuff matters

How about this? Have you ever gone into a restaurant and been able to smell their cleaning solution throughout your meal? I appreciate that they have disinfected the table after the last guy left, but I don't want to smell the disinfectant. You may be saying to yourself that I need to eat in better restaurants. Actually I eat in great restaurants, but sometimes a guy has to have a chicken-fried steak or some barbecue and that doesn't come from places with tablecloths or carpet—you need Formica and linoleum.

More little stuff that matters:

> *Paper on the restroom floor, or worse, no paper*
> *where there is supposed to be paper.*
>
> *Crumbs on the floor.*
>
> *Chipped paint on the doorjamb.*
>
> *A rumpled shirt on an employee.*
>
> *An employee with body odor, greasy hair, or nasty shoes.*

A quick, gross story that makes my point: I love to eat mussels. At least I *used* to love to eat mussels. My family and I were in a great little seafood restaurant where I ordered a bucket of them. The waiter, who provided great service, smelled so bad that I finally held a wedge of lemon under my nose every time he came by the table. It ruined the entire dining experience. I have never been to that restaurant since then. More important, and the things that ticks me off most, I haven't eaten a mussel since that day. The experience had such a profound effect on me that I forever lost my appetite for what had been one of my favorite foods.

All of this so-called little stuff is an indication of how much respect you have for your company, your customers, and each other. And as my little story proves, they have a lasting impact.

"Yeah, but you don't understand our business. We manufacture . . . We distribute . . . We aren't an office-type environment . . . We . . ."

Let me make this clear: I don't care. The little stuff matters. No way around it. My opinions of your business make a difference in how much I trust you and whether I am willing to share my money with you.

Easy fixes

Don't allow employees to smoke outside the front door of the business. Your front door is the opening to the "cathedral" of service, not a smoke hole.

Insist on clean desks. No excuses. Regardless of the fact that people say a dirty desk is just their style, it's a lie. A disorganized workspace means disorganized work habits. A sloppy work environment equals sloppy results.

Dress like you are going to work. Look your best. Casual Fridays were a terrible idea. Jeans day is stupid in an office environment. Productivity suffers when people don't dress to the top level of the position they hold.

Fire anyone who openly disrespects another employee, a customer, or your workplace.

Larry's short list on respect:

- *Build respect in your organization from the ground up.*
- *Respect your coworkers, especially in front of customers.*
- *Respect your customers, especially in front of other customers.*
- *Respect your competitors, especially in front of customers.*
- *Respect the physical space your business occupies.*
- *Remember that little stuff makes a big difference in how customers perceive your business.*

CHAPTER 9

One big happy family . . . yeah, right!

I am always skeptical when business owners or managers tell me their organization is just one big happy family. These people are either blind or stupid. It doesn't take five minutes of walking around among the employees to know that many of them are not happy at all. And it takes only about that long to know they don't like their brothers and sisters and they hate Mom and Dad and they think their cousins are all inbred bozos.

How happy is your family? Don't lie. How happy is your family all of the time? The truth is, your family is dysfunctional. That's okay; all families are dysfunctional. In that way alone is your company like a family.

Your organization is not one big happy family. You work together. That's it. No more and no less. With family, you pretty much have to put up with one another. At work, it's a different story. In your family, your mother may make you go to your idiot brother-in-law's birthday party. At work, your boss shouldn't make you do that. In fact, let's talk about the whole birthday party, wedding shower, baby shower, and she-had-a-mole-removed party thing. I'm sick of them. Aren't you? Why should you be expected to celebrate the birthday of a coworker when you know your life would be better if he or she had never been born? But instead, we take company time to circle up in the break room to celebrate every occasion known to man or woman. Why? Do that on your own time if you are so inclined. Don't make those who don't want to participate feel bad because they don't want to play along.

So am I against friendships at work? Not at all. I have found that most of my friendships have come from those I work with. But that does not mean I have to be friends with everyone I work with. So don't expect me to.

We are not a family. We are not related. I don't have to like you. I don't have to spend my time with you. I just have to work with you. That's all I have to do—everything else is a matter of choice.

You are required to tolerate the person you work with to the point that the job (that thing you are paid to do) gets done. Everything else is a bonus.

Can't we all just get along?

The answer: Sure we can. In a perfect world we can all get along perfectly. Do you live in a perfect world? I don't. My world has just never been perfect, regardless of how much I want it to be. My world is full of people I find very hard to get along with. In fact, I don't even want to get along with them most of the time. My world is full of idiots.

You still have to work with the idiots. Sadly, you don't have a choice. That is also part of the job. The world, and therefore the workplace, is full of idiots. And the reality of life is that when you get rid of one idiot, another will show up to take his place. It's the curse of humanity. The only thing you can do is learn to spot them and know how to get along with them as best you can. I didn't say you have to learn to like them—for me, that has proved to be impossible. I just said get along with them.

There are all kinds of rules for getting along with other people; I am going to give you a few of mine. But before I give you my rules for getting along with the idiots, you need to be able to identify them.

Let me give you what I am positive is an incomplete list of idiots. I admit it is incomplete, because as soon as I identify all the types I know, someone will offer me a new type.

The Liar. My dad always said to me that it is better to have a thief than a liar working for you, because at least you can watch a thief. I have never forgotten that. Consequently, I can't tolerate someone who lies to me. In fact, as a manager when I find that someone has lied to me, I fire him. Period. No questions asked—no room for negotiations. I suggest you do the same. Harsh? Not at all. Lying is a character flaw that destroys trust, and when you can't trust the people you work with, you are doomed. And it doesn't matter how small the lie is. A lie is a lie is a lie. And a person who will lie about the small things will also lie about the big things.

The Cryer. Well, boo-hoo to you, too. Sorry, but women have this one pretty much to themselves. And that's not being sexist; it's just a fact. I have had thousands of employees throughout my life, and I've never had a man cry about his job. The best thing to remember when it comes to business is what Tom Hanks said in the movie *A League of Their Own*: "There's no crying in baseball!" Well, there's no crying in business, either. Crying is nothing more than a form of manipulation. Yes, I know, sometimes it is an honest emotional reaction to a significant, upsetting occurrence. A coworker hurting your feelings doesn't count as a significant upsetting occurrence. Neither does getting a bad performance evaluation. If you get a telephone call that your house just burned down or your dog just got run over or someone close to you died, then you can cry. I may even cry with you. Other than that: Big waah! Get over it and move on.

As a manager, if someone sits in front of you and cries, hand them a box of tissues and wait patiently for it to end. Don't fall victim to this unfair act of manipulation. Even if you sincerely sympathize with their plight, stay tough. This is a business you are running, not a kindergarten.

Mr. Happy. Mr. Smiley. Mr. Positive. Mr. Every-Cloud-Has-a-Silver-Lining. Mr. There's-a-Light-at-the-End-of-the-Tunnel. Mr. I've-Got-a-Cliché-for-Everything. Got a picture of this guy yet? I have renamed this guy: Mr. You-Make-Me-Sick. Sometimes you have to wipe that stupid smile off your face and get a big ugly frown on it and go to work! Sometimes the light at the end of the tunnel is a train. Every cloud does not have a silver lining. Sometimes it is hiding a hurricane. "Hey, Mr. Positive—you can be positively stupid, positively lazy, and positively wrong!" Regardless of what the motivational speakers tell you, attitude is *not* everything, attitude is only one thing; sooner or later you have to get off your butt and go to work!

Am I knocking being positive? Absolutely not! However, I am saying there are many people who spend more time being positive than they do getting the work done. Sometimes you don't want Mr. Positive Attitude. Sometimes you actually want Mr. Crappy Attitude who is sick and tired of the incompetence and the slacking off and wants to get some real work done. He has a bad attitude and wants things done right now in the right way with no questions asked. In that scenario I'll take Mr. Crappy Attitude over Mr. Positive Attitude every time.

Susie Sweetheart. She's so sweet, you want to puke. Know her? Sure you do. Beware: I have been stabbed in the back by little Susie probably more than any other type of idiot. She can fool you. And Susie Sweethearts come in both sexes. They are so sweet and caring and want to be your best friend . . . to your face. Don't turn your back.

The Bully. Bullies come in all shapes and sizes. In business, they aren't the big guys like on the playground when you were in elementary school. Sometimes the business bully is the little gray-haired receptionist who has been with the company forty years. Sometimes it's the guy who is in charge of the supply room who makes sure that you never have any staples. Sometimes it's the boss.

Bullies have fragile little egos and can't find power through their talent, so they use whatever else they have at their disposal. In the case of the bully boss, it's their title. "Do what I say because I'm the boss." Pay no attention to the fact that it makes no sense, just do it because he said so. How do you deal with them? The same way you dealt with the bully on the playground: You confront them. Bullies almost always back down when confronted. The key thing is not to be afraid of a bully. Bullies thrive on fear and will run from confidence. Just be firm and logical, don't lose your temper, and in case you get fired, have some money in the bank.

The Gossip. This person knows everyone's business. They don't normally get much work done because they are so busy finding out everyone else's business. They spend a lot of time on the phone, they wander around a lot, and they get tons of e-mail. Remind the gossip that you pay them for their results, not their information. And never reward a gossip by listening to their gossip. That's why they gather information—to pass it on. Don't play into their schemes.

The Ass. This one has some subcategories.

The Smart-Ass. This guy always has a smart-ass remark to make. When done in good humor it can relieve a lot of tension, which is a good thing. But when it's done in a mean, sarcastic way that doesn't move anyone closer to the goal at hand, this person is just an irritant.

The Hard-Ass. My wife, Rose Mary, once worked for a woman who had a reputation for being the company hard-ass. She knew it and was proud of it. She was a workaholic and lived, ate, and breathed the business. She was at heart a nice person but a total pain in the butt at the same time. She embraced that about herself and wore it like some badge of honor. At a party one night, she was more or less bragging about it. Being the shy and retiring person I am, I asked her why she was that way. She gave me the "company" speech—that this is a business and that people should be focused on putting as many pagers (remember pagers?) on the street as possible and that she expected everyone to care about it as much as she did and yada, yada, yada. I told her, "Hey, they're pagers. Mostly doctors, drug dealers, and nerds wear them. I can buy one off a card table on the street corner just like I can buy one from your big company. This isn't world peace or starving children we are talking about—it's pagers! Lighten the hell up!"

I don't think she understood me at all. Then again, I didn't understand her, either. You can care about your company, be passionate about your company, love your company, and love what you do, but lighten up and don't be a hard-ass.

The Kiss-Ass. This person is easy to recognize; he's the one with brown on his nose. This is usually the nicest person in the whole place—everyone's best buddy. Just wants everyone to get along and be friends, and thinks that every idea is a brilliant one. They want to be liked. They want to make everyone happy. They constantly tell you what a good job you are doing, how smart you are, and how much they admire you and enjoy working with you. Watch out for this person. He is probably an insincere suck-up who says nasty things about you behind your back.

The Dumb-Ass. This isn't just a convenient thing to call someone; it's actually a category of idiot at work. These poor folks are just inappropriate. They say dumb things, do dumb things, and God love 'em—there's just not much that can be done about them. Put up with them and hope you don't have to count on them too much.

The Cute-Ass. You know this person: too cute for her own good, certainly too cute to get much real work done. These people are just trying to slide by on their cuteness. And this is not just a female thing either. There are plenty of pretty boys out there who are sliding by on their perfect teeth and perfect hair and six-pack abs. Am I jealous? Yeah, just a bit! I was never able to get by on my good looks. I had to have results. So should everyone!

So am I against hiring hotties? Not at all. And not all hotties are bad employees. I am just saying that at work, people should be judged on their results and not on how they fill out their jeans.

The Jackass. This is the person who has no respect for anyone else's opinions, ideas, words, actions, work, personality, or job title—and shows it. If this person works for you, fire him; life is just too short to have a jackass working for you. If you work for a jackass, quit and go to work somewhere else: Life is too short to be disrespected by a jackass. If your coworker is a jackass, transfer if you possibly can. If you can't, distance yourself in any way you can. You should also make it clear that you will not tolerate him being an ass to you. If that fails, quit and go to work somewhere else. Again, life is just too short.

"I get the point, Larry, so what should I do?"

Idiots are self-absorbed. They don't care about you and they don't care about the company. These people have one interest: themselves. They have fragile egos that need to be fed. They are the way they are at home with their families and with the few friends they probably don't really have. However, my advice is this: Don't give them the attention they so desperately crave, regardless of the lengths they go to in demanding it.

Idiots usually have a very selective memory. Write stuff down. The person with the best notes wins. If you are in a confrontational relationship with an idiot, always protect yourself with good documentation.

Don't let it get emotional. Don't let the idiot get under your skin. Easier said than done, I know. But you let idiots get control of the situation the minute you get upset, and then they have won. When you give them a piece of your mind, you give up your peace of mind.

Don't avoid an idiot. Idiots must be dealt with. This isn't hard for me—I like confrontation. I have no trouble looking someone in the eye and saying, "You are an idiot and I'm not going to tolerate it." Most people are not confrontational. In fact, most people would rather do anything than have a confrontation. But it must be done. Otherwise, change your name to Matt and prepare to be walked all over. Suck it up and address the problem. Confront the idiot in a calm, businesslike manner. In other words, call them on their stuff. This is not in conflict with the previous statement of being calm. This is just making sure that the idiot doesn't get one over on you and feel superior based on your ignoring their stupidity. I don't believe stupidity should be ignored. I believe you have to deal with it, call it like it is, and then move to quickly get past it.

Idiots are manipulators. They manipulate ideas, stories, facts, and relationships. Again, call them on it, even when the manipulator is your boss. I suggest a closed-door session in which you lay it all out. This is tricky and it may not leave you in the best situation, but it must be done to retain your own sanity and personal integrity. On the other hand, if the manipulator is your employee, tell her that her tactics are not going to fly around you; let her know you are onto her and will show no mercy in dealing with her.

The single universal rule for dealing with idiots:

Never reduce yourself to their level: That's where they want you. Rise above them. When they get mad, either ignore them or laugh in their faces, but don't fight with them. Don't play their game. Remember, they invented the game and when you sink to their level to play it, they will win.

As my buddy John Patrick Dolan, lawyer, speaker, author, TV personality, and negotiations expert, always says, "When you fight with a pig, you both get dirty . . . but the pig likes it!"

The ugly truth: sometimes you are an idiot too

Yes, you are—don't bother defending yourself. Every single one of the traits I have talked about currently exists somewhere within you. Maybe not to the point where the trait manifests itself daily, but occasionally it will show up. You have manipulated, you have been a bully, a whiner, a crybaby, a yes-man . . . all of them. The good news is that if you are aware of the categories, you can identify these traits within yourself and take corrective action quicker.

It's okay to mess up

Have you ever made a costly mistake? Have you ever really messed up? I have. I have also had employees who have messed up badly. I had a guy who worked for me who screwed up a lot. His nickname was Cowboy. When I left town on a business trip, I always left him in complete control. I would give him a list of things that had to get done while I was gone. That list became the Holy Grail to Cowboy. He plowed into it like you wouldn't believe, and his tasks always got done. His methods weren't always pretty, but he got it done. However, he made a lot of mistakes. The thing that saved him every time was that when I got back in town, he would come into my office, shut the door, and tell me that the work got done but that he had made some mistakes. He would immediately fall on the sword and tell me what he had done wrong. He would tell me how he had lost his temper or made someone mad or in hindsight he wished he had done something differently. He always took responsibility for his actions.

That is the ultimate lesson when you do something stupid. Take responsibility for what you did.

As a manager, when one of your employees comes to you and says, "I'm an idiot. I messed up and I'm sorry," praise his honesty—this is a good person. Few people will ever do this.

Crap happens

Sometimes things just go in the dumper. Hey, you've heard it before in slightly more descriptive language: Crap happens.

What to do when it goes in the dumper:

1. Apologize for the overall results. It's hard to argue with a sincere apology.

2. Clarify all of the reasons it didn't work out the way it was supposed to.

3. Take responsibility for your role in these reasons. Take full personal responsibility for what you did without taking the full blame for the whole thing unless the whole thing was entirely your fault. This is the time you point out that you played a role in the results, but there were other factors. This is not the time for finger-pointing or blaming others. This is an honest assessment of all that went wrong and how you played a part.

4. Have a plan to fix it. Always. Never walk into your boss's office and throw the problem in her lap with an attitude of "There it is—it's your mess now." And never have a "save me!" attitude. Instead, have a fix-it plan. Have ideas on how to get out of the mess. This is where you move the discussion to the solution and away from the problem. Good leaders are more interested in solutions than problems. This action alone may save your bacon.

Once an idiot, always an idiot?

Usually. My experience has proven to me that idiots are always going to be idiots. This is both a good thing and a bad thing. The bad thing is that you can't fix these people. If you understand this early in the process, you can save yourself an enormous amount of time, agony, and energy. The good thing is that idiots are totally predictable. You know how they are going to react and respond in advance in most situations, so you can make allowances for it. Even if their particular idiocy is unpredictability, that can be predicted.

One of the things I have learned about dealing with all people is this: People change—but not often. People change only when they want to, not when you want them to. Most idiots are oblivious to the fact they are idiots and therefore never see the need to change. Even when it is pointed out to them, they don't get it. Idiots are usually blind to themselves.

And another thing that I want to address that doesn't seem to fit anywhere else:

Sexual harassment, my ass

"You look nice today."

"You look great in that outfit."

"Did you get your hair done?"

"Is that a new perfume? I like it."

"Great shoes!"

"Hey, Jimbo, lookin' good!"

That is not sexual harassment. Those are compliments. Remember those? That's when someone says something nice to you simply because they want to say something nice to you. Or they genuinely admire something you are wearing. Or how nice you look.

At most, statements like those might be considered flirting. You remember flirting, don't you? It's when people say something nice to you because they find you attractive. They might want to eventually ask you out. They might find you the kind of person they want to spend more time with. They might just like you and want to be nice to you.

But those statements and a million more like them are *not* sexual harassment. "Hey, baby, want to join me in the supply closet so we can bump uglies? And by the way, if you don't, I'll fire you." *That* is sexual harassment.

An inappropriate remark about body parts is sexual harassment. Unwanted touching is sexual harassment. You know what it is. In fact, as I have learned about most things in life, when you have to ask yourself whether something is or isn't, chances are you already know. For instance, know a dirty joke? Sure you do. Ever ask yourself if the timing was right to tell it? Did you look around at the crowd, consider who was there and where you were and ask yourself if you should haul out your new dirty joke? If you did, then you already knew the answer to the question. The fact that you had to ask proved that you know when something is appropriate and when it's not. The same applies when it comes to this stuff. If it's truly sexual harassment, you will know it. Kind of like the Supreme Court's position on pornography.

Is this legal?

I'm not a lawyer and I didn't consult one before I wrote this. So don't hold my feet to the fire on this stuff. I'm not being legal here. Besides, most of this shouldn't be about the law. This is all just common sense. Just use your head. And please—lighten up, people.

If someone flirts with you and you aren't interested, just say so or give the signal that you aren't interested. Just like you would in a bar, at the gym, on the street, on an airplane, or at church.

If someone says something that you find offensive, say so. Confront the situation and be very clear in your communication so you aren't misunderstood. Start off by keeping it between the two of you. Most things can be handled quietly and amicably by just clearly stating how you feel. You know how to do this stuff—don't turn simple flirting into breaking the law. Just handle it like a grown-up!

In many cases, remember that old saying "Ignore it and it will go away." Learn to let the stupid stuff slide. Don't pay any attention to it—don't put any energy in it and it will usually disappear. In other cases, laugh it off. You'll know when it's serious and you will know when something really needs to be done about it.

If someone says you look nice, do what you should do anytime someone says something nice to you. Say, "Thank you." If someone grabs your ass and you didn't invite it, then go to the boss and report it. By the way, notice I said "and you didn't invite it." Don't invite it, flirt back, tease back, and then be surprised when someone takes you up on the offer. Again, just use good common sense.

To the women:

Ladies, men are idiots when it comes to dealing with women. We think with the wrong head almost all of the time. You confuse us, confound us, and intimidate us. Our mouth and brain don't work in sync when we are around you. We say stuff that to us sounds perfectly innocent and complimentary. Please, if you don't like it, just let us know. Set us straight. We will probably be astounded, as we are all so ignorant about these matters. So tell us, wait for our humble apology, and forgive us . . . please.

However, many men are not just idiots about such matters; they are snakes and will say whatever it takes to get what they want. You know the type; chances are a snake has bitten you before. However, you will also be able to recognize us because there are plenty of women who are just as reptilian as we are.

Just remember this rule: People are people. Some are genuine and nice and fun and flirtatious and well-meaning. Some are stupid, manipulative jerks. Welcome to the world of people.

Sometimes we get along too well!

Sometimes you will have a genuine, honest attraction to someone you work with. It happens. You will be tempted to date a coworker, your boss, or even an employee. When it happens, what should you do? There are many who would say that dating a coworker is a definite no-no and should be avoided at all costs. You should probably listen to those people. Breakups are a disaster and can ruin a good working relationship. On the other hand, lovebirds have a tendency to make most of us want to puke, and the workplace just isn't the place for all of the energy it takes to create and sustain a goo-goo-ga-ga romance. So all of the books and advice and company policies that say office romances should be avoided are absolutely correct. Heed that advice.

On the other hand, I found the love of my life at work. I was her boss's boss. It broke all of the rules of the company we worked for and was a bad idea in every way. But we fell in love and it worked out. We didn't hide it at work. We kept it in check. If the company had said that we needed to quit because we were dating, either of us or both of us would have quit because the relationship meant more to us than the job. Therefore I am not the best guy to give advice on avoiding office romances. I believe that jobs come and go but finding the love of your life shouldn't be passed up. I barely remember the job I had twenty-five years ago. My wife is still with me and always will be.

Am I condoning office romances since I've had one that worked out? No, I still think they are a bad idea. But we are people. We are usually led by our emotions, not our brains. Whether you have office policies stating that it absolutely cannot happen, whether you know it's a bad idea or not, it is still going to happen. People are going to be attracted to each other. That's just the way it is. Be smart about it. Don't let it get in the way of the work. That's the key. Everyone was hired to do a job. If the job gets done, the rest can be dealt with. However, if the job is not being done, then the relationship must be addressed.

I'm about the work. Are things being sold? Is the customer being served? Is everyone contributing to the bottom line? Are people getting along well enough to get the work done? If so, what else really matters?

Larry's short list for dealing with idiots:

- *We are all dealing with stupid people. It's not a comfortable boat to share, but at least it's a boat we are all in.*
- *Never reduce yourself to their level, because that's exactly where they want you to be. Rise above them.*
- *Mind your own business. Do your job and leave the idiots to themselves as best you can.*
- *Confront and communicate. Everything is dealt with better when it is out in the open.*
- *Be fair, because everyone has a bad day. Determine whether it's a bad day or consistently bad, inappropriate behavior.*
- *Give people a chance. Not many chances, but at least a few.*

- *Don't be a tattletale. Don't always run to the boss with every little infraction you see unless someone's welfare is at stake.*
- *Your coworkers are not one big happy family; you don't have to like them. You are required only to tolerate them, and anything more is a bonus.*

CHAPTER 10

Ethics: it's black or white

We live in a society bathed in gray. I don't believe in gray. I think life is either black or white. It's right or wrong, good or bad; you are either in the way or on the way; it is hello or good-bye. We have learned to walk a fine gray line in gray little offices where things aren't quite wrong but they aren't really right, either.

Ethics is not a sometimes thing. It is something that makes itself evident in all areas of life and business at every moment of the day, from taking only fifteen minutes on your fifteen-minute break to the disasters of Enron. Ethics is more than a list of do's and don'ts by which we conduct our business. Ethics is the kind of people we are, the kind of people we hire and fire, and the way we think. It's the core of our being and the core of our business.

The old idea that you can't get a good deal from a bad guy

must be understood and exploited. The bad guys must be identified and held accountable, and the consequences must be enforced.

What's unethical?

Calling in sick when you aren't.

Taking company office supplies.

Lying on your résumé.

Getting a haircut between sales calls.

Fudging on an expense report.

Saying a product will do something that it won't.

Being late for an appointment.

Making personal phone calls at work.

Using company phone lines to make long-distance calls.

Using the company copier for personal copies.

Overpromising and underdelivering.

Using the company postage machine for personal mail.

Disparaging a competitor.

Participating in office gossip.

Taking a long lunch hour.

Not returning a phone call.

Not checking your voice mail as often as you should.

A recent study by Kelly Services said that 31 percent of employees think it's perfectly fine to use the company Internet for personal use during work time. Sorry, it isn't.

The same survey said that 14 percent of employees think it's okay to take office supplies home for personal use. No, that's called stealing. It isn't right. All 14 percent should be fired.

Interesting to me that the same survey said that 53 percent of employees are satisfied with their employer's ethical standards.

If the employer knows that employees are stealing office supplies and surfing eBay and writing personal e-mails using the company Internet and are letting them get by with it, the employer doesn't have many ethical standards. Evidently most of their employees approve of that. I know I made quite a leap in logic there, but I am entitled because it's my book. But you get my point: People steal from their employers by stealing paper clips, software, pencils, and more. They steal from the time they were paid to do their work by doing personal business on company time. Call it what you want, but I call it unethical and stealing.

Does all of this sound like I am a "company guy"? Yes, I am. I have owned a few companies and I've even gone bankrupt because I made stupid mistakes and let things slide when I shouldn't have. I don't believe in letting things slide any longer. It takes a toll. Someone always suffers.

"But everyone does it, Larry!"

I used to say that to my mom when I was a kid and wanted to do something when she had told me that I couldn't. Her response was always, "If everyone was jumping off a building, would you do it too?" It ticked me off when I was a kid, but she was right. The behavior was wrong—I knew it was wrong—but I still wanted to do it. Besides, not everyone was doing it. Just a few. So the fact that some do it and get by with it doesn't make it the right thing to do or the smart thing to do. You can drive with your feet, but that doesn't make it a good idea!

There is also the matter of personal ethics

You know in your heart whether something is right or wrong, and you do what is right simply because it is right. It is a matter of integrity. Refuse to ever compromise your personal integrity. Even if your manager asks you to do something you think is wrong, stand your ground. You can get a new job, but you can't get your integrity back.

I tell a story in my speeches about Sonic Drive-In. I'll tell you the whole story a little later in this book when I talk about customer service. I love Sonic and have eaten about a million (that's a lie, by the way) of their cheeseburgers. In the story, Sonic was running a special that I wanted to take advantage of, but the special featured Pepsi-Cola. I have a line in the story that says, "I hate Pepsi." About half of the audience will usually applaud when I say it because, like me, they are Coke drinkers. The other half will boo because they are Pepsi drinkers. It's a risky line for someone in my business. I work for many food groups, fast-food chains, and restaurant associations where

Pepsi is either in attendance or sometimes even a sponsor. I know some are worried that when I use that line, the Pepsi people will be offended. They are probably right. But I am comfortable with the fact that because of that story I am never going to be Pepsi's convention speaker of choice, just like they aren't my soft drink of choice.

At one meeting where I had been hired, a few minutes before I went onstage I was told that Pepsi was one of the sponsors but Coca-Cola was not in attendance. They asked me to please change my story to say "I hate Coke" instead of "I hate Pepsi." I said to them, "Surely you aren't asking me to lie, are you?" They couldn't believe I took it that way. They said they were just trying to make sure their sponsor was not offended, and what did that have to do with lying? I told them that I didn't hate Coke. I loved Coke. And to change the story to say I hated Coke would be a lie because it wasn't true and it didn't happen that way. I told them I would tell it the way it really happened or I wouldn't tell it at all. They wanted the story but just wanted me to tell it differently, they said. I told them I wouldn't do it and would just drop the story entirely. Now, some would say they were the customer and I should have just changed that one word for that one speech and then moved on. I disagree. I believe I served my customer well by demonstrating to them I would not compromise my integrity. I felt better for having done it. They learned I had integrity, and I reminded myself that I wasn't a sellout.

So how do you know when it's right or when it's wrong?

I do a couple of things to know whether something is right or wrong. The first thing I do is to ask myself, "Would I want my mother to know about me doing this?" Silly? I don't think so. I might disrespect myself, but I would never disrespect my mama. If I wouldn't want my mama to see me doing it or to know about it, then I don't do it.

Then there is always this idea, which I have always found to be extremely effective: If you have to ask whether it is right or wrong, it's wrong. Just having to ask the question gives you the answer. If it is the right thing to do, you know it without ever having to question it. Just trust your gut.

Larry's short list on ethics:

- *Ethics is not a sometimes thing.*
- *Anyone who will lie about the little things will lie about the big things.*
- *Any time you give less than your best effort, you are stealing.*
- *Listen to your gut; it knows right from wrong even when the rest of you can't figure it out.*
- *If you have to ask if it's wrong, it is.*

CHAPTER 11

How to absolutely destroy the competition

I've got your attention now, don't I? Chances are you even looked at the table of contents and skipped to this chapter because you want to know how to annihilate your competition. Don't feel bad; all businesspeople want to know how to absolutely destroy their competition. Everyone is looking for the one big secret of how to do just that. Okay, I've got the one big secret.

You destroy the competition
when you stop believing in it.

Bummer! You are disappointed, aren't you? And now you think that after all the practical advice I have given you up to this point in the book, I am going to get all New Agey and woo-woo on you. Right?

Wrong. I am giving you the most practical advice on competition you may have ever received. Stop believing in the competition.

The more you believe in it, the more power you give it to destroy you. Forget the competition and instead focus on yourself. Stop making your winning about them and start making it all about yourself.

The smartest thing I ever said:

"Discover your uniqueness and learn to exploit it in the service of others, and you are guaranteed success, happiness, and prosperity." —LARRY WINGET

Yep, that's it: the smartest thing I have ever said. That one line sums up my whole approach to business success. Why? Because no one can compete with your uniqueness.

Once an individual or a company discovers their uniqueness and learns to exploit it, they will be successful. No one can compete with a truly unique individual or company. I don't believe much in competition, but I'll bet my money on uniqueness.

How do you know what your uniqueness is? Here is a hint: It probably isn't what you are doing right now. Few individuals or companies are currently following their unique path. Instead, they are trying to play like everyone else; to fit in; to look like, act like, and be like all of the others. They play "me too" to the point where it is almost impossible to tell one person from another or one company from another. In response to that, people and companies make it their goal to become different from everyone else. Bad idea again.

Don't be different. Different scares people. People won't spend their money on different. They will, however, pay a premium for unique.

Think Apple. Are they different? I say no. They sell a computer that does what most all computers do. They all do about the same thing. But Apple is unique in the way they do it. Their computers don't look like other computers. They come in colors and strange shapes. That uniqueness has pulled them successfully along for a long time. Each generation of their computer offers something better than the last. And the iPod? Get out of here!! In my humble technological opinion, the iPod and TiVo are both technology at its finest.

I spoke at the annual meeting of a computer printer manufacturer a couple of years ago. I sat in the meeting for nearly two hours before it was my time to go onstage. I listened to the director of manufacturing, the vice president of sales and marketing, and the president of the company all spend their time trashing their competitors. They laughed about their competitors' products, made fun of their leadership, and led their own sales force in cheers about destroying each one of their competitors. I thought to myself that this company was doomed. They spent no time talking about how their product was technically superior or how their customer service was better or how their salespeople were better trained. They didn't spend a

minute on how they were going to go from fourth in the marketplace to number one. They didn't have a clue about what
made them unique. Instead, they spent their entire meeting
tearing down the companies that were obviously doing a better
job than they were doing. When I took the stage, I had to make
a decision. Do I bother telling them how wrong they are, or do
I just do what I do and move on? I hadn't been hired to com-
ment on their belief system, so I just gave my standard remarks.
Plus, they were too far gone. Gone from the top down and the
bottom up. They had created a culture of tearing down instead
of building up. You never build yourself up by tearing others
down.

Know what? Their market share today is just about what it
was a few years ago. I am not surprised.

Enough about me, let's talk about me

The key to winning is never about them losing, it's always about
you winning. Your winning is not about "them." It's about you.
You should focus on becoming the kind of company that no one
can compete with. I like what my friend and futurist Dan Bur-
rus says: "Focus on competition has always been a formula for
mediocrity." Rise above competing and instead be unique so
that you have no competition.

"How easy is that to do?"

It isn't easy at all. That's why so few succeed at doing it.

You know what I'm talking about. If you read many business books, you know *exactly* what I'm talking about. It's called **branding**—one of the hot new buzzwords in business. I hate buzzwords. They are double-talk and do nothing but hamper clear communication.

Branding is nothing but knowing who you are and what you do that makes you stand out from everyone else, then communicating that through your marketing efforts. Branding is discovering your uniqueness and learning to exploit it.

I am a brand. I worked hard at establishing that brand. At a time when most professional speakers were broken into only two categories—trainers on a given subject or motivational speakers—I created my own category: Me!

I have trademarked the term The World's Only Irritational Speaker® to position myself in opposition to all of the motivational speakers out there. I have also trademarked The Pitbull of Personal Development®, which I believe clearly identifies who I am and what I do.

I wasn't always as clear about who I am—at least not on the outside. Early in my career I was pretty much like everyone else—a motivational speaker who could do some sales training, customer service training, and leadership training. I was nice, encouraging, supportive, and positive. I made myself sick. That is just not who I really am. I am caustic and irreverent, and I believe that your life is always your own damn fault. But I wasn't selling that, because I was convinced that in order to be successful I should do what everyone else was doing, but just be better at doing it. That is a clear formula for disaster in both my business and your business. You won't always be better at doing what needs to be done. You should try, but the bottom line is that you simply won't always be. However, you can always be better than anyone else at being who you are. That's the real key.

I learned this years ago when a meeting planner was talking to me about my speech on leadership entitled "The Eight ATEs of Leadership," which contains my eight principles for becoming a better leader and makes up part of the leadership chapter in this book. She told me that she wanted to hire me to speak to her association, but another speaker they were considering (one of my best buddies) had a speech on leadership that contained ten principles. Since mine had only eight, they were going to hire him instead. I decided then and there to stop competing based on the content of what I had to offer, because someone could always have one more principle than I have on any subject. Instead I decided to become so unique, no one would buy me based only on what I had to say, but would instead buy me based on how I said it. No one can say things exactly like I say them. It was simple: I just let go and became who I really am. No one can compete with who you really are.

No one does Larry Winget like I do Larry Winget, though many have tried. I have fully embraced my uniqueness. I am fine with being an in-your-face, abrasive personality who just tells it like he sees it. Why? There is an audience who wants that and is willing to pay a premium for it. You are reading this book, aren't you? I have learned that when I fully embrace my personality, no one can compete with me, nor should they try. It's a brand that wins and a marketing concept that can't be beat.

You have a brand that will win in your business too. Maybe you don't know what it is. But you must find it. Why? When you do, no one will ever be able to compete with you.

Look at your business. No one has your exact location, your exact employee mix, and your exact attitude. Others may sell the same product at the same price right next door to you, but they still can't be you. You and your business are one of a kind.

Abandoning who people think you are and becoming who you really are is a simple concept, but sometimes it is very hard to do. It isn't easy to give up others' ideas of who you are. Yet the key to success is to discover your uniqueness and to exploit it. Your authentic persona, either personal or corporate, is the key to your prosperity.

Sorry, it's too late

You have already been branded. Before you get a chance to even do it, it's already been done. Your reputation did it for you.

You might be known as a good guy. That's not a bad thing. You might be known as a good guy who does good work but is really slow. That's not such a good thing. You got that reputation because of the work you have done in the past. As a result you became branded as the good guy who does slow work.

Companies and organizations have reputations too. Some are known for speed: FedEx. Some for quality: Mercedes-Benz. Some for customer service: Nordstrom. Some for being cool: Apple. Some for being slow: the post office. Some for being idiots: the government.

Take a look at Southwest Airlines. Entire books have been written about them. Southwest Airlines is fast, fun, and cheap. You know clearly in advance what you are going to get. It is their reputation, and they live up to it at every turn. It works for them. I think they are amazing.

How do they do it? How can Southwest Airlines empty a plane and reload it in less than fifteen minutes when it takes other airlines forty-five minutes? They want to. They want to turn a plane quickly, so they do it. Plus, they include you in the process.

I recently took a short flight from Phoenix to Las Vegas. The plane was running about fifteen minutes late. The gate agent got on the loudspeaker and told everyone he knew they wanted to get to Las Vegas on time and those with connections wanted to make their connections with plenty of time. He said the only way that was going to happen was if they all pitched in and worked together to load that plane in record time. That meant finding a seat and getting in it fast—just sit down, shut up, and get it done. Everyone laughed and happily did what they could to get the plane out of there on time. And we did leave on time.

On the other hand, I recently took an American Airlines flight that was also running about fifteen minutes late. When I approached the gate agent to ask what the new arrival time would be, she told me they would get the plane loaded in fifteen minutes and be out on time. I asked her who she thought they were, Southwest? She didn't laugh. Of course it took nearly an hour to deplane and get the plane reloaded. By the time we finally took off they were already making announcements about what to do if you missed your connection.

Many would say that the difference is that Southwest doesn't have assigned seats and that is why they can unload and load a plane in fifteen minutes. I disagree. That plays a part, but the real reason is the attitude of the airline and the employees. Southwest's goal is to run an on-time airline. Each employee tries to do that and they enlist their customers in the process. The entire airline plans for success. They know who they are, their customers know who they are, and they involve everyone in the process of living out who they are.

The other airlines seem to plan for failure. They have developed an entire culture of excuses. They don't expect it to work, and it doesn't. I watch the airline executives on television talking about how they just can't seem to be profitable. And that's even after the government gave them all of that money after 9/11. Have you seen those interviews too? They don't have a plan to be profitable. Oh, I know they have a written document about exactly what they plan on doing in perpetuity. But they haven't included everyone in the process; it hasn't become a part of their culture. And they didn't include their customers. Instead they took away the blankets, the pillows, the magazines, and the food, and in the process they developed a bad attitude to make it all less palatable to the people with the money: you and me. Are they surprised that many of us have a problem with them? They didn't get us on their side. They didn't make us care about their success. They treated us badly and played takeaway with us, and then copped an attitude when we complained. They got an attitude and then expected us to happily spend our tax dollars to bail them out. Screw 'em. The government didn't bail me out when I took a hit after 9/11 and it probably didn't come to your rescue either. I learned to run a better business and to cinch my belt a little tighter just like most others did.

I find it amazing that Southwest Airlines can literally throw a bag of peanuts at me and I am tickled to death, yet the other airlines can give me a first-class meal and I am disgusted.

I recently told an American Airlines flight attendant that the only thing being Executive Platinum did for me was get me on the plane earlier so they could be rude to me longer. Again, I was the only one of us who thought that was a funny line.

There isn't one airline out there that really competes with Southwest Airlines. Sure, there are other low-cost airlines that fly the same routes and at pretty much the same fare. But it isn't the same experience you get when you fly Southwest. It isn't an apples-to-apples comparison. Love them or hate them, you can get what they have to offer only from *them*.

That's what you should be trying to do. Make yourself unique so they can get the experience you offer only from *you*.

It can be done lots of ways.

Your colors can set you apart. UPS is brown. They have made it a part of their culture. Brown.

Geico does with it with a lizard—a cute little computer-animated lizard. They expanded that with the whole "I've got good news, I just saved money on my car insurance" campaign.

Progressive Insurance does it by giving you a Web site where you can check their rates against the rates of their competitors. Their competitors are even sometimes cheaper. A gutsy move I admire.

Domino's Pizza used to say that their pizza would be delivered in thirty minutes or it would be free. Were they selling pizza or speed? Trust me, they were selling speed. After a few years of selling speed and evidently giving away too many free pizzas because their drivers were having too many traffic accidents, they have abandoned that policy. Now they are back to selling pizza. I think they might be in trouble.

DHL is now saying that they are putting customer service back into the shipping business. I love that ad campaign. They know we all think the other big two who ship things are totally devoid of customer service, so they are setting themselves apart by saying they have what the others don't: customer service. Do they promise faster service or better pricing? No, they just promise better service. I like it. As a result of that ad, UPS is now making a real effort to do better in the area of customer service, something UPS seems to have let slide in the past. Yet they are responding to the market's response to a company that decided to take something we all expect (customer service) and make it uniquely theirs. Cool.

"You were placed on this earth to create, not to compete."

—DR. ROBERT ANTHONY, author, *Beyond Positive Thinking*

Look at who you are. What is your history? What have you been through that no one else has been through? What lessons did you learn? What do you do that no one else does? What *could* you do that no one else does? What is there that is so uniquely you, that you could exploit in the service of others? It's there. I promise. Discover it. Use it. And you will never concern yourself with the competition again.

Larry's short list on competing:

- *Do not believe in the competition.*
- *You cannot build yourself up by tearing others down.*
- *Customers won't spend their money on different, but will pay a premium for unique.*
- *"Branding" is just discovering your uniqueness and learning how to exploit it.*
- *Your uniqueness is always based on your authenticity.*

CHAPTER 12

The eight ATEs of leadership

Normally, I hate little bits like the one I am about to give you. I am not into acronyms and parables and cuteness in any way. But I like this little list of things that a leader can do that all end with the letters "A-T-E." I like it because making all the words rhyme makes the points easy to remember. That's enough of a plus for me to be a little cute this time. Forgive me.

CreATE

You must create three things as a leader:

1. The right environment.
2. The right atmosphere.
3. The right group of people.

Create the right environment

Seems simple enough, doesn't it? But what can you really do about the physical environment? A lot. I don't care whether corporate built you a big box that looks like every other store in your chain. I don't care whether you run a lawn-mower repair business out of your garage. I don't care whether you have a thousand cubicles that all look alike. As the leader, you are responsible for making sure that the physical environment of your workplace is inviting and clean, and shows that this is a place where business takes place and that customers can trust you. That can't be done if there are a handful of employees who have turned your front door area into the smoke hole where they take their break. It can't be done if the floor is dirty or if you have restrooms that aren't clean. It can't be done if your break room has a refrigerator bursting at the seams with spoiled food. And it can't be done when you have people just standing around.

A poor physical environment affects employee attitude and employee behavior. It affects the attitude of customers toward your business, too. Clean up the place. Take down all the goofy crap on the walls of cubicles. Clean out the fridge. Get rid of the smoke hole. Then watch more work get done.

Create the right atmosphere

The leader must create an overall atmosphere of personal accountability.

One where employees understand that every action has a consequence. The leader has to enforce those consequences, and, in fairness to the employee, these consequences must be known clearly in advance. This atmosphere of personal accountability is not a negative atmosphere. In fact, it's a very positive atmosphere that promotes good service and allows good employees to rise to the top. One where people who do a good job get recognized for their performance.

The leader must also create an atmosphere where people are allowed to think freely, offer suggestions, and be creative. Most leaders think they should tell people to keep their noses to the grindstone and never look up. Some jobs require that the nose remains stuck to the grindstone, but most don't. Besides, if you must constantly make sure that your people keep their heads down and stay busy, you (1) have the wrong people and (2) are managing the process, not leading the organization.

Create an atmosphere where thinking is rewarded and held in high esteem and new ideas are encouraged.

Create the right group of people

"The speed of the leader determines the speed of the pack."

—SGT. PRESTON OF THE YUKON

Hire right. That's tough, I'll admit. Résumés don't tell you much, and legally, former employers can't tell you if your prospect is an ax murderer or a thief—they can only confirm that he worked there. Plus, it's become really hard to legally ask "telling" questions any longer. Add to that the huge number of people who are great at BS, and what do you have to work with when hiring? Not much—except your gut. And even your gut can be fooled. I have been fooled many times. Some people are just great at being interviewed. I call them "articulate incompetents." The best you can do is talk to the person, get a feel for who he or she is, ask the best questions you can (there are many books out there to help you with this), then follow your gut.

Make it your goal to hire good people. I remember a very old ad for the hotel chain owned by that pillar of good business ethics Leona Helmsley. She said in the ad, "We don't teach our people to be good, we simply hire good people." Great idea. I am amazed she came up with it, considering she did jail time for fraud. But even if she didn't originate the statement and some ad agency made it up, it's still something we should all shoot for. You can, for the most part, teach someone how to do a good job. You can't teach someone to be a good person. Hire good people and then train them to do the job.

When you get a good group of employees working for you who share a common goal, there isn't much that can't be done.

Larry's 20-60-20 principle

I believe that everyone in your employee pool fits into one of three different categories:

The Top 20 Percent

These are the cream of the crop. They get to work on time, do their job, have integrity, are honest, have respect for their coworkers and customers, and work hard whether you are around or not.

The Bottom 20 Percent

These are the people who are the exact opposite of the top 20 percent. They are worthless to you, your organization, and your customers. They may be nice people, but you aren't paying them to be nice people; you are paying for results. These people don't have the results.

So what are you left with?

The Middle 60 Percent

These are the people who are "pretty good" at their jobs. They do most of what they are supposed to do. For the most part, they are good people and they are good employees. Not great employees. Not really bad employees.

What does the 20-60-20 principle mean to you?

From a management standpoint, understanding my principle will make your life much easier.

Manage the Top 20 by staying out of their way. Just check in with them to find out what they need in order to do their jobs and then give it to them. These employees don't need any hand-holding. They certainly don't need you looking over their shoulders. They need your support and encouragement and that's about it. After all, these employees do their job regardless. They don't complain; they just get things done. Let them do it.

But know this about the Top 20: They will leave you eventually. They will move on and leave you standing in their dust. These employees need a constant challenge, and even if you provide it, they will eventually have to move on to bigger, better, and newer things. It's in their DNA.

Now to the Bottom 20. We have been conditioned to work with our poor performers. What a load of crap. Write them off. Save your energy. The Bottom 20 are like the old cliché about teaching a pig to sing: It can't be done, and it irritates the pig. It is a waste of time and energy. It's impossible to do. You can't motivate the unmotivated. You can't educate the ineducable. You can't make someone care. Give up. Get new people instead.

Spend your time instead with the Middle 60. These are the people who need your help and deserve your time and energy. What is your job as a leader? Easy. It is to move the Middle 60 into the other two categories: the Top 20 and the Bottom 20.

That's right. Your goal is to move the middle toward the top *and* toward the bottom.

This is reality: If you walked into your company tomorrow and fired every single employee in the Bottom 20, it would take almost no time at all for your Middle 60 to split itself and drift down to fill the bottom rank. In fact, many of them have been waiting for the opportunity to do just that. They wanted to be at the bottom, but until you got rid of the people who were already there, there was never any room for them, so they just kept their heads down and did "pretty good" work. But now there is room for them, and they will gladly move into the Bottom 20. This is great news for you. Why? Because you know exactly what to do with the Bottom 20: Fire them!

It works the other way too. If you walked into your company tomorrow and every one of your Top 20 had left you for bigger and better things, then it would take almost no time at all for people from your Middle 60 to step up to the top rank. Yes, the same idea works at the top, too. You actually have amazing employees in your middle rank who can't wait to be in the Top 20. There just wasn't any room for them, so they didn't show their stuff until they needed to.

That's why your time must be spent with the big Middle 60. It is a gold mine of talent just waiting for a chance to shine. It's also full of losers just waiting for their chance to be slackers. Your job is to identify which direction your employees are headed in. That way, you won't be upset when one of your Top 20 disappears, because you will already know that you have someone ready to step up and take her place. Don't panic—just promote. On the other hand, you will also know who is going to be a bottom dweller, and you can begin the process of sending him on his way.

You can fire people all day long and the percentages will stay the same. You will always have a Top 20, a Bottom 20, and a Middle 60.

"May I kneel and kiss your ring?"

This concept can save you so much time, money, and heartache that I fully expect leaders and managers to run up to me and fall at my feet in adoration. Yes, it's that powerful. Understanding how it works can change the way you spend your time at work every day. It can save you money. It can actually make you money. It can lighten your load and improve your outlook. It is the be-all and end-all of business management! Am I getting carried away? Okay, but you still owe me big-time for this one. It is *the* way to manage your workforce.

CommunicATE

The first thing the leader must communicate is a common goal for all to follow. Communicate the big picture.

Do you, as the leader, know what the big picture is for your organization? And don't give me the old company line "It's to make money." Every business has a goal of making money, even though not many do a great job of it. And please don't rattle off your mission statement. I have seen few mission statements worth reading. Nine out of ten say the same meaningless things:

To serve our customers yada yada yada, to maintain profitability yada yada yada, to treat each other with respect yada yada yada. Most mission statements are nothing *but* yada yada yada!

I say if you can't explain what you do for a living in one sentence, then you don't know what you do for a living. The same is true for most companies. If you can't explain what your company does in one sentence, then you don't know what your company does either.

What do you do for a living? Really. Tell me. Say it out loud right now. Did you say it in one sentence? No? Work on it until you can.

What does your company do for a living? As the leader, you should be able to say it in one succinct sentence. That sentence is your statement of purpose. Have you communicated that sentence to everyone in the organization?

Some say that your statement of purpose, your mission statement, and your one sentence should be some lofty idea that encapsulates your higher calling. Bull. No one will understand it, care about it, or know how to accomplish it.

Have you ever heard the story about the guy who walks up to three bricklayers who are working on a building and asks them what they are doing? In case you haven't, let me finish the story:

The first guy says, "I am just putting in my eight hours until I can go home."

The second guy says, "I am laying bricks."

The third guy says, "I am building a cathedral."

The doofus motivational speaker who told you that story undoubtedly told you that only the third guy really understood his calling. Only number three had the big picture.

Only number three had a higher purpose. What a load of total crap!

There are times when the best of us are doing nothing more than just putting in the hours until we can go home. There are also times when we just need our employees to lay bricks. What's wrong with that, anyway? After all, the employees were hired to lay bricks, so encourage them to be great bricklayers and lay the damn bricks! It's what they were trained to do, it's what they are paid to do, it's what needs to be done. So do it. It's always honorable to do what you are paid to do and get done what needs to get done.

Besides, the guy who said he was building a cathedral was supposed to be building a Wal-Mart Supercenter.

I have been around those types who are always "building cathedrals." Sometimes their head is so far up in the clouds, they don't lay their bricks straight. Employees don't always need a higher calling. Sometimes it doesn't matter what the purpose is, we just need to have the bricks laid.

Okay, enough of the metaphor; hopefully you get it by now.

Communicate what the job really is

Many employees don't make their employers happy because they don't know what to do to make their employers happy. No one told them what their job was. Yeah, they were told "you are the janitor," or "you are a salesman," or "you are the company president," but they still had no idea what that entailed.

Get every person in every job a job description. Articulate what must be done, when it must be done, and most important, why it must be done. Give them a personal mission. Make it an action statement they can get behind and work toward. If you get enough people to understand and accomplish their personal mission, then fulfilling your company mission will take care of itself.

When communicating what needs to be done, don't spend much time telling people how to do things. Instead, focus on explaining to people what to do and why it needs to be done and then let them surprise you with their creativity. A *why* is always more energizing than a *how*.

Don't assume that everyone understands what you are saying. Learn to communicate in a clear, concise manner.

Great leaders use strong language. And I don't mean they cuss like sailors. (By the way, why do sailors always get the credit for being good cussers? I don't think that's fair to the rest of us great cussers out there!) I mean that great leaders speak in absolutes. No one has to wonder what a great leader thinks. She says it clearly, concisely, and with confidence.

Sadly, our ears have become so sensitive thanks to all of the political correctness in our society that we automatically assume that anyone who can actually give an opinion is rude. Wrong. Never confuse clear, direct, candid, even blunt communication with rudeness. Learn to appreciate people who can get a point across quickly and effectively with no room for misunderstanding.

"I think your results might possibly improve if you would consider trying to accomplish your task in this manner instead of the way you are currently going about it."

Huh?

"Hey, you're messing up. Don't do it that way. Do it this way."

Gotcha. Now I understand.

EducATE

I was hired to speak to a door-installation company. They had a room full of guys in do-rags, with lots of tattoos, and many were drinking beer at nine a.m. I thought I was in trouble. Don't get me wrong—I felt right at home with these guys, I just wasn't sure how this crowd at this time of day under these circumstances would respond to what I had to say. The company thoughtfully had bought everyone in the audience a copy of my book *Shut Up, Stop Whining & Get a Life*. I really respected what this company was doing. They were investing in the results of their employees.

When I went onstage these guys gave me a round of applause that few speakers ever receive. When I finished, they were standing in their chairs cheering me. They stood in line for more than an hour to have their books personalized. This meeting wasn't for the managers. This meeting was for the workers—the people who actually hang the doors and see the customers every day. This company had it figured out. They had put their money where their mouth was—in the front-line employees, the guys who get them the results.

Education is not the same as developing potential. It is not the job of a leader to develop potential in others. It is the job of the leader to hire people with potential and then stay out of their way so they can use their potential. Besides, there is no time to develop people. Today we are forced to do more with less, and the best way to do that is to hire and keep only the best employees.

Spend your time and money educating those employees who

possess potential. Those who don't possess any potential shouldn't even be working there.

"Don't the employees who do not have potential need the education more?" Sure they do. So run a charity and give it to them. Running a business is expensive and takes time. Remember: You don't have the time or the money to educate people who don't have potential.

Encourage your employees to go to seminars, take courses, read books, listen to audio seminars, and watch DVDs of seminars and speeches. You should spend time helping them become the best people they can become. Educate in life skills as well as business skills.

I believe that every company should have a learning/lending library that contains educational material. Not just stuff about the job (people can almost always figure out how to do their jobs when they are trained properly), but material that teaches people to be better people. There are great books out there on how to set and achieve goals, and audio CDs and DVDs that teach this skill as well. Answer this question: Would your employees be better at their jobs if they knew how to set and achieve goals? Of course they would. That skill has nothing to do with the technical information required to do their jobs; however, we all know they would be better at their jobs if they possessed that life skill. How about fitness? Would your company be better off if your employees were fit and focused more on health? Sure they would. And it would save you money. Healthy employees don't take sick days and don't cost as much from an insurance standpoint, and they do better work because they feel better. Is that a business skill? No, it's a life skill with amazing results for your business.

Few companies encourage life skills improvement. They don't seem to understand that good people produce good results. So teach people life skills.

Remember that obtaining these skills is ultimately the responsibility of the individual. Employees can't be made to become better people. That is a personal choice. Companies, however, owe it to themselves to make the opportunities available. If your employee wants to go to a particular seminar, offer to split the cost with him. Or if you read a great book that you believe would benefit your employees, buy one for all of them. (Feel free to start with this one.) Education is expensive but not as expensive as uneducated employees.

"Train everyone lavishly; you can't overspend on training."

—TOM PETERS, author, *In Search of Excellence*

Practice what you preach

As a leader, you should also read the books, go to the seminars, listen to the CDs, and watch the DVDs. You should then share what you have learned. Set the example for others.

Do me a favor. Right now write down the last five books you read in the past year or are currently reading. You can even start by writing down this one.

1. _____

2. _____

3. _____

4. _____

5. _____

Did you come up with five? If you did, then good for you. If you didn't come up with five books, then you are a lousy leader. Sorry, no slack for you and I mean what I say: You are a lousy leader if you can't come up with five books you have read about life and business over the course of an entire year. You might manage the work process well, but you aren't leading your people to a better place.

"But, Larry, I'm busy! There is no time to read." You have just made the wrong excuse to the wrong guy. There is always enough time to do what is important to you. You aren't reading because it isn't important to you. Make personal and professional development important enough to dedicate some of your time every day to this goal.

"Setting an example is not the main means of influencing another, it is the only means." —ALBERT EINSTEIN

DelegATE

You don't send a Porsche to pick up the trash.

It costs too much. It's not built for it. It would take too long to get the job done. Instead of a Porsche, you send a trash truck. It's the appropriate vehicle for the job and can do the job better and faster and more appropriately. It is built for it.

The same applies to effective delegation. The leader shouldn't do work that should be done by someone else. Someone who is cheaper. Someone who is faster. Someone who does it better. Someone who likes it more. Those are the rules of delegation. If it can be done cheaper, faster, better, or by someone who likes it, then let them do it.

One more time

Before you do something yourself, ask these questions:

Can it be done cheaper? In other words, by someone who is at a lower pay scale?

Can it be done faster? Some people are just faster at doing certain tasks than you are.

Can it be done better? Even though you are the leader, someone else might be able to do some of your tasks better than you can. Let them. Prove that you are smart by getting the job done by someone who can do it better than you.

Can it be done by someone who likes it more than you do? You don't have to love every task. Believe it or not, there are people who enjoy firing people. I was like that. So I became the guy who fired people, because I enjoyed it more than my boss did.

ParticipATE

You don't have to know how to do the job, but you better know what it takes to do the job. At one point I owned a telecommunications company that sold and installed business telephone systems. I was great at making sure they were sold, but I had no clue what it took to get them installed. So from time to time I would promise things to customers that just couldn't be done. That was a horrible mistake. My installation manager would go crazy when I promised things that he and his crew couldn't do. So I got an education in what it took to get those telephone systems installed. I watched what happened after the system was sold. I went on site surveys and watched my installation crew wire a building and install the jacks and program the system and hang it on a wall and plug in the phones and test them. I learned what it took to do each of those things, and I was a much better leader because of it. Did I know how to do it? No, but I knew what it took to get it done.

> *"No good decision was ever made in a swivel chair."*
> —GEN. GEORGE S. PATTON

Reward the behavior you want repeated. Reward the behavior you want to see others emulate.

Larry's guidelines for rewarding people:

- **Do it immediately**. *Don't wait for the company meeting at the end of the month. When you see an employee do something "reward-worthy," stop and reward it. People should be rewarded in the same ways dogs are trained. When you train a dog, if your dog does something right, you stop and have a party. When the dog does something wrong, you give it a short, quick correction.*

- **Make the reward specific**. *Don't say something general like "You are doing a great job." That doesn't mean anything and doesn't reinforce the behavior you would like to see repeated. Instead, say something like "I like the way you handled that customer when you told them blah blah blah." The more specific you are and the more immediate you are in pointing it out, the more likely you are to see the behavior repeated.*

- **Praise publicly as well as privately.** *If you reward immediately and specifically, most of your rewards will go unnoticed by the other employees simply because they won't be around to see them or hear them. That's okay. You might embarrass some people by making a big public display of their daily accomplishments. And you can unmotivate others by praising one person too much. But some accomplishments do warrant public praise and should be repeated at your next meeting so all can learn from what happened. So make it public when appropriate.*

- **Be creative.** *I read a study that said the most important thing to people is free time. So how about giving an* employee a two-hour lunch as a reward? Or for something really outstanding, how about the whole afternoon or maybe an entire day off? That's a creative way to reward someone, and I guarantee it will be appreciated and noticed. You can also reward with an education day, where you send a deserving employee to a sales seminar or other seminar being held in your area. Give a book, a CD, or a DVD. It's not hard to be creative in your rewards, and it can be a fun way to get employees involved in their own reward system as well by asking them what they would appreciate.

- **Keep the reward positive.** Please don't steal the thunder by saying something like "Good job; I guess you can keep your job another month." Or something even worse like "Jane did a great job this week. Why can't the rest of you do your jobs as well as Jane does?" You just made Jane the bad guy to all of her fellow employees and ruined the reward by turning it into a punishment for her outstanding accomplishments. If you do this, don't expect to see Jane do outstanding work again. No one wants to be used as an example like this.

- **Make the reward personal.** Employees are like your kids; you can't treat them all the same. You take one to the park to play ball; the other one you take to the mall. One gets ice cream and the other wants a steak. Know your employees well enough to reward them with something that is meaningful to them. You might have someone who loves flowers. Give them a nice bouquet. Someone else might love to read. Buy them a book. Don't give the book person flowers. See how easy this is?

I have a friend who owns a company of about a hundred people. He is a big, loud, gregarious guy who believes strongly in personal accountability. His favorite thing to do is to catch someone doing something right and then hand them a hundred-dollar bill. He is also a big believer in personal development and reading. He loves walking up to people and asking them what they are reading. He then asks them what they liked best about the book to prove to himself that they were actually reading the book. Then he hands them a hundred-dollar bill. Tell me who doesn't appreciate a crisp new Benjamin? He told me that after a few months of doing this, it became hard to find someone who wasn't reading a book or working hard to get caught doing something right.

By participating in the rewarding of your people, you prove to them that you are involved in the entire process: not just when things go wrong, but when things are going right.

HibernATE

Okay, you've done everything I've suggested. You have delegated, communicated, educated, participated . . . all of it. Tired? You should be. Now it's time for you. Get away from it all. Seriously. Walk away for a little while. Go see a movie in the middle of the day. Close your door and take a nap. Take off a few hours early and go home and play with the kids.

"But I could never do that!!" If that is your response, then you haven't really done all of what we have talked about. You haven't trained your employees to function on their own. Any company that requires constant supervision is not a well-trained, well-managed, well-led company. If you can't slip away for at least a few hours, you have been a lousy leader and have not done your job.

Besides, your employees need a chance to do their jobs without you around. This is the "get the hell out of the way" part of the job. You have to trust that you have done your job and that your people can function without you. Don't be that overprotective mommy who won't let her kids walk to the school bus when they are fourteen years old. Step back.

I spend a good amount of my time on airplanes. I constantly see people on their cell phones, barking orders and checking up on their employees right up to the point that the flight attendant stands over them and insists they hang up. Then the instant the plane's wheels touch the ground, they fire up that cell phone and call back, picking up midsentence where they left off. If I cared enough to talk to these people, I would guarantee that most would defend their actions by saying that they are only "staying on top of things" back at the office. They would be convinced they cared enough to do a good job and remain involved even when they were traveling. The truth is, they are lousy managers who either didn't train their people well enough to take care of things or don't trust their people to be able to act without constant supervision. I think many of them are sad, pitiful people who are so ego driven that they think only they can actually make a good decision.

Learn to step away. Force yourself to take a little time off, even if it's just a few hours. Even if it's just taking enough time to walk around the block or to go out for coffee. Trust your people to do what they know how to do. Let them surprise you.

Even if they mess up, it will give you something to work on when you get back, and you will actually have the energy to work on it.

EvaluATE

You have given your employees a chance to perform the job they were hired to do and paid to do. Now it's time to evaluate their performance. Don't just assign a task and expect it to get done. Please don't be so naïve as to think that the work will get done just because it's supposed to get done. You must inspect what you expect.

Evaluate these two things: activity and productivity.

I am not a big supporter of busywork. However, I am even less of a supporter of people just standing or sitting around doing nothing.

When I was in the telephone business, I had a telephone installer who would pick up a broom and sweep the warehouse when he was between installation jobs. It wasn't his job to sweep the warehouse, and when I would periodically remind him of that, he would always respond with "I know that, but it's not my job to just stand around, either. You pay me to work, so I'll work." Did that go a long way with me? Duh! Would it with you?

Activity, while not the most important thing to evaluate, is the easiest to evaluate. It's not hard to see whether the work is getting done. Look around; check a few reports and figures and you pretty much know.

The most important thing to evaluate is productivity. It is more than just getting the work done; it's getting the right work done, the right way. It's not "Is the work getting done?" as much as it is "Is the job getting done?"

Evaluating productivity will take a little work on your part. Evaluating overall productivity requires investigating individual performance.

Let me point this out to you again: I said "performance." That is the only thing you have the right to evaluate. You don't have the right to evaluate the performer, only the results. I have had people work for me whom I just didn't like. Who cares? They got the job done, so what difference does it make if I like them or not?

There is an exception: You have the right to critique the performer if it has an impact on the performance. If the person is such a jerk that customers and coworkers don't want to be around him, you have every right to point that out. If the person is annoying to the point that it affects the way others interact with him and less work gets done, it is your obligation to point it out and take action on it. If you don't approve of her lifestyle choices or his religious affiliation or you don't like her hair, tough—it's none of your business. Ask yourself these questions: Is the work getting done? Is it getting done the way I want it done? If the answer is yes, reward them for it and move on. The rest just doesn't matter.

Constructive criticism: a stupid concept

How dare I call constructive criticism a stupid concept! It is an excellent management tool! Nay, nay, naïve one! Think about it. Construct means to build up. Criticism means to tear down. You can't do both at the same time. If you want to build people up, then take the time to do it and do it well. Encourage them. Point out their strengths. Tell them all of the good attributes they possess. Then send them on their merry way. If there comes a time when they mess up—and they will mess up, because we all do—then criticize their performance. Point out what they have done wrong and teach them how they could have done it better.

Many authors and trainers suggest that you sandwich criticism between praise—like feeding someone a "shit sandwich." The nicer ones, not me obviously, will call it a "praise sandwich." I have never appreciated it when someone has tried this silly technique on me. It's insulting. Just tell me what's on your mind, either good or bad. I'm a big boy. I can take it.

If someone taps you on the shoulder and offers to give you a little constructive criticism, get ready for your sandwich. Even if they serve it up with cinnamon raisin bread (my favorite), the main ingredient is still shit. Just say to them, "If you want to be constructive, I'll happily listen to you. If you want to criticize me, get after it. Which one is it going to be?"

The real danger of feeding someone the sandwich is that you run the risk of the criticism getting lost amid all of the praise. When the criticism is lost, the lesson is lost as well and the entire experience has been a waste of time and energy and just leaves a nasty taste in your mouth.

Keep it simple. Praise when it is appropriate and critique when it is appropriate. Remember the lesson from dog training I mentioned earlier? When people do well, you have a little party. When they mess up, you give them a short, quick, immediate correction. In both cases, you move on.

Besides, what is wrong with criticism? Don't shy away from it. Never forget that it's your company, your department, your customers, and your money at stake. You have every right to be critical of the way the people you are paying are doing their job.

Desire vs. ability

When evaluating people and their performance, ask yourself these two things about the employee:

1. Does the employee have the desire to do the job?

2. Does the employee have the ability to do the job?

What you will find is that most of your employees have the ability to do the job. Fewer will have the desire.

I would almost always rather have someone who was a ten on desire but a one in terms of ability. I can teach just about anyone to do almost anything—therefore ability has never been much of an issue with me. If people have a sincere desire to do something, they can usually be taught to do it. However, if someone has no desire, what difference does it make if she is great at doing something? You can take a person with all the ability in the world, and if he has no desire to do the task, it's just not going to get done.

At one time my wife was the manager of a telecommunications company. She had a wonderful employee working in the customer service department who desperately wanted to become an outside salesperson.

Rose Mary gave this first-rate employee the job of outside salesperson, but the employee promptly became a disaster. She couldn't make a sale. She couldn't manage her time or territory. She became discouraged, started showing up late, and her attitude went in the dumper. The problem: great employee in the wrong job. The fix: send her back from whence she came. Yes, it was hard to do. It was embarrassing for her because she had to admit she wasn't good at something she really wanted to do. It was hard for Rose Mary because another person had already filled the former job. But she got it done because really great employees are not easy to find, and they are worth some inconvenience to protect and keep.

This person had the desire to do well, but not the ability. As a manager, do your best to match the desire to do the job with the ability to do the job. Then you have someone who will accomplish great things.

Some of the time, you will have employees who have neither desire nor ability, and don't much care about acquiring either. What do you do? Easy!

AmputATE

I watch a lot of television shows about animals. I like Jeff Corwin and all those other strange people on Animal Planet. Years ago, I watched a show about catching monkeys. The monkey catchers put out glass jars with peanuts in them. The jars had small openings at the top, but fairly large bottoms and were made of heavy glass. When the monkeys showed up and reached down into the jars to grab the peanuts, their fists full of peanuts were too big to get back out through the small openings. The monkeys were caught. For fear of losing his peanuts, a monkey wouldn't let go of the nuts long enough to pull his hand out, leaving himself trapped and captured. I guess he was afraid that there would never be any more peanuts, so he had to cling to the ones in his hand.

Many managers and leaders are the same way. They are so afraid of losing the people they have that they end up trapped. I guess they are afraid that there will never be any more people to choose from, so they have to cling to the people they've got out of desperation and fear. Sad, isn't it? There are plenty of nuts to choose from. There is not one person who can't be replaced. There are plenty of very capable individuals out there who would just to love to work for you. People who will jump at the chance to do it just the way you want it done. People who are willing to work hard, show up on time, follow directions, and serve your customers well. But chances are you will never find those people and those people will never find you, because you aren't willing to fire the people you already have who aren't doing their jobs.

The solution? Relax your grip and let these people go. Cut these people loose. Amputate!

One of my managers was once having a really hard time making the decision to fire one of her employees. I asked her why this was a problem for her. She said, "I just don't want to do this to him." I was astounded by her answer. This bozo was a horrible employee. He was usually late, always rude, wasn't good at what he did—just a bad hire in all respects. But the manager was having a problem amputating this guy from our organization. I then reminded her that firing is not something you do *to* someone; firing is something you do *for* someone.

> *Firing is not something you do* **to** *someone:*
> *firing is something you do* **for** *someone.*

Yes, you read it right. Firing someone actually does the employee good; it is done for his benefit. The person getting fired doesn't fit into your organization. His skills don't match your opportunities. His attitude doesn't match what you are trying to accomplish. He isn't playing the same game you are playing. He isn't moving you closer to where you want to be; instead, he is moving you farther away.

Let these people go so they can find a place where they do fit in. Do you think they don't know they aren't a fit? Trust me, they know. Whether they will admit it to themselves or not, they know they aren't a fit for your organization.

So stop thinking you are hurting the employee. You aren't. You are actually helping the employee go someplace where he will be happier and more appreciated. Someplace where his skills match the opportunity offered.

I will admit that many you set free won't see it as a favor. Many will be totally pissed that you are firing them. Oh, well. That's not your problem. Your problem is getting them packed up and out the door. It's not up to you to make them understand or agree with you. You don't have to defend your position or argue with them. Just tell them why you are firing them. Have your reasons well documented, then do the deed and walk them to the door and wish them well. Then go hire someone to take their place.

Look at your organization. Do you have people who should be fired? What are you waiting for? Cut them loose!

"But they might sue me!" You are right; they might. We have become a big sue-happy society, and it makes me sick. Gone are the days when, as the owner of a company, I could walk in and say, "You suck at your job, you are an idiot, you are a liar, you are a thief, you piss me off just looking at you— you're fired." Man, I miss those days! Now there are rules that must be followed. You can't just fire people because they can't do the job. You have to document it, give multiple warnings, and offer counseling—all kinds of stupid, expensive, wasteful stuff.

Get me straight here; I am not suggesting that you break the law when I tell you to fire someone. Do what you must according to the law and the rules of your company. But I still believe this: It's better to spend money on a really good attorney than a really bad employee. You're better off fighting them on the outside of your company than from inside your company.

*It's better to pay a good attorney
than a bad employee.*

No bad employees

Seriously. I promote the idea of having no bad employees. Is that unreasonable? Of course it is. In fact, it's impossible. It goes back to my 20-60-20 Principle. Even if you get rid of the bottom 20 percent, there will be a group ready and eager to take their place. There are always going to be bad employees. But you don't have to employ them—at least not for long. Either fix them or fire them. Don't tolerate them for one minute more than you have to. To hell with all of the stupid laws that protect those who are unwilling to work. Your business is too important to put it in the hands of the incompetent. Your customers are too important to turn over to people who don't give a damn. So dump the bad employees as quickly as you can. Do it, all the while knowing that you will immediately have more bad employees to deal with.

The old cliché "It's my way or the highway" is true. The company has the right to decide how it should operate. Your employees have the right to go away if they don't agree with it. The company has the right to help others expand their opportunities by holding the door open for them to go away.

I have a good friend, Dr. James Kohner, a periodontist who runs a successful practice in Scottsdale, Arizona. He made some changes in the way he ran his office, and many of the employees held a mini-revolt protesting his changes. His response, in my opinion, is classic: "Don't forget, it's *my* name on the door." Amen.

Bad employees are killing your business

Bad employees hurt the customer. Funny that anyone would allow the very person who keeps your company alive and prosperous (the customer) to be hurt by a bad employee, yet it happens every day. Never allow the customer to be hurt by anyone at any time or in any situation.

Bad employees hurt other employees. When you tolerate poor performance in an individual, you are sending the signal to other employees that it is okay to behave poorly or to do a less-than-spectacular job. After all, the boss condones it, so what difference does it make, right? When you refuse to accept anything but stellar performances from all, then you have a much better chance of receiving stellar performances from all.

Bad employees hurt your credibility as a leader and manager. Every employee in your organization knows who the hero is and knows who the goat is. It's not a secret who is skating by and slacking off. You lose the respect of every employee when you tolerate the slacker. You don't even have the respect of the slacker! Earn the respect of all by taking the appropriate corrective action by either fixing or eliminating the bad employee.

"Okay, okay, let's get to the firing!!!"

Or . . . Don't let the door hit ya where the good Lord split ya.

You know I am a proponent of getting rid of people who don't contribute to the success of the operation. So let's talk some about how to do it.

No surprises

I would like to make this clear: If firing someone comes as a total surprise to them, then chances are, you need to be fired as well. You have to make sure you have warned bad employees that the consequence of their actions may result in their dismissal. That way, the firing won't be a surprise. To let employees think they are doing fine because you haven't been doing your job as a manager by talking to them about their performance is just unacceptable. To fire an employee under those circumstances is also unacceptable. Of course, there are times when something happens and immediate action must be taken and the employee must be walked out the door on the spot—but those occasions are rare.

Larry's list for firing people:

- *Communicate. Explain what the problem is, make sure they understand your position (not agree, just understand), and then let them know that the consequence for continuing the unacceptable behavior is dismissal. If it happens again, remind them of the previous conversation and send them on their way immediately.*

- *It's about results. Always make the reason for termination— or for any disciplinary action you take—about results. You pay for results, so stay focused on that. Don't make it personal and don't let the employee make it personal. Focus on results and performance.*

- *Do it quickly. Don't threaten it or drag it out. Letting employees hang around even for a day after they have been given notice can be very destructive. They can steal from you, drag down the morale of others, and do all kinds of tacky things to hurt you and your company. Fire them and walk them to the door immediately.*

- *Don't argue. If you are at the point where the decision has been made to terminate the employee, then there is no need to argue about it with the employee. State your case, do the deed, and walk her out the door.*

- *Have a witness. Because we live in such a sue-happy society I also recommend that you take notes. Documentation and a witness can save you lots of money and legal problems. Give the employee severance if you are so inclined.*

> ■ *Make all new hires "at will" employment. This is a great little thing that can keep you legal in most matters of termination. Make sure that when you hire people, they know their employment is "at will," meaning you can fire them at your discretion. Put it in their employment agreement. Oh, and check with your attorney first. Don't get sued on my account.*

"But, Larry! You forgot one! What happened to motivate??"

First of all, if I added motivate, I would have to call this the Nine ATEs of Leadership, and it just doesn't have the same snappy ring to it as the Eight ATEs of Leadership. Second, I don't believe in motivation. That's why I am not a motivational speaker. There was a time when I did call myself a motivational speaker—along with another 5,000 professional and nonprofessional speakers. Then I realized that I have never succeeded in motivating another person to do anything. You haven't either. That's why I became The World's Only Irritational Speaker®. I am convinced that I can't motivate you to go from where you are to someplace better; but I will guarantee you that I can make you so irritated with where you are, you will do anything to be someplace better.

Follow my lead and become an Irritational Leader. A leader

who demands excellence to the point that if your employees aren't willing to give it, they will become so irritated with you that they will run from you and your company. Make it your goal to have standards so high that only the best and the brightest will be willing to work for you. All others will go to those companies with lower standards.

Remember it is not the job of the leader to motivate others. It can't be done anyway, so don't waste your time. Motivation doesn't work. You can threaten, coerce, dangle money, time off, and carrots of every size, shape, and color and it will always come down to this: People do what they want to do when they want to do it and when the consequences of not doing it are painful enough to force them to do it. Got it? Let's move on.

Larry's short list on leadership:

- *Management is about* how *the job gets done; leadership is determining* what *the job is and moving people toward getting it done.*
- *Remember 20 percent of your people are terrific, regardless of what you do. Twenty percent of your people are horrible regardless of what you do. Spend your time helping the remaining 60 percent.*
- CreATE *the right physical environment, atmosphere, and group of people.*

- CommunicATE *clearly the big picture to employees.*
- EducATE *the employees who possess potential, including life-skills improvement.*
- DelegATE *if something can be done cheaper, faster, better, or by someone who likes it more.*
- ParticipATE *by being an active part of the process and rewarding desired behavior.*
- HibernATE *occasionally to let employees do their jobs on their own.*
- EvaluATE *activity, which will be obvious, and productivity, which is trickier.*
- AmputATE *bad employees, remembering that firing is something you do* for *them, not* to *them.*
- *Motivating others is impossible—forget it.*

CHAPTER 13

Teamwork doesn't work

Shocked? Astounded that I would dare say that? Ticked off because your team means everything to you?

Tough. Teamwork doesn't work. I'm right about this; everyone else is wrong.

Amazon has more than 46,000 books that contain the word "team" or "teamwork" in the title. They say you can't run a successful business without great teamwork. Those books lied. Yes, you heard me right: They lied. People who have never actually owned a company must be writing most of those books. If they had actually run a business, they would know that teamwork doesn't work and that they are lying to people, trying to sell them on an idea that is a waste of time.

Maybe you have even been involved with companies who hire very expensive "team" consultants who create elaborate games and exercises to teach people how to work together as a team. Maybe you have participated in a ropes course or a jungle safari or played jacks with your coworkers to figure out how to work together better. You probably had a good time and some laughs together, but I promise you didn't go back to the office and work together better as a team—at least not for long.

Teamwork doesn't work
because someone on the team won't work.

There is no way around it; someone won't do his part, so the whole concept of the team doing the work falls apart while someone else has to pick up the slack in order to get the project finished. Then you have lots of resentment.

You know that I'm right. Chances are, *you* have been the one picking up the slack for some lazy slacker. Want to know why I know that you are the good guy in the equation? You are reading this book. The slacker is too busy doing nothing and dodging work and responsibility to actually read a book. (I'm getting smarter with every sentence, aren't I?)

There is no "I" in team

I am always amazed that this stupid cliché adorns so many posters and shows up in offices around the country. Some people even put on their company smiles and get out their banners and give little speeches at their company meetings around this ridiculous notion.

There really is no I in team. There is a T, an E, an A, and an M. No I. That's why it doesn't work. It is the lack of an I that tells us all exactly why teams don't work: It is never about the team, it is always about the I. People want individual recognition and couldn't care less about the team. And if you honestly don't agree with that, then I know exactly what kind of an employee you are. You are a mediocre performer who likes to hide among the many instead of being recognized for your individual talents, because you don't have many individual talents.

"There is no I in TEAM, but if you jumble it all up, there is a ME." —GREGORY HOUSE, MD, from the Fox TV series *House*

The answer?

Instead of teams, we should create groups of superstar individuals who share a common goal. Then you allow those superstars to exploit their uniqueness in an environment where other superstars are doing the same thing. This mutual respect for the talent of others helps them achieve the common goal faster and allows them to excel as individuals, which is better for their egos. It takes care of the whole "what's in it for me?" mentality that we all possess, because the individual doesn't have to share the credit with people who didn't contribute. Regardless of what you have been told, people don't really like to share. Can I have a bite of your chocolate? There, see?

We still have to work together

Superstars with a common goal must still work together, and happily will if there are other superstars whose talents and abilities they respect. Superstars love working with other superstars who are great at what they do. But this is not teamwork. This is a common goal being accomplished by a group of individuals who have individual tasks, are held accountable for their tasks, and are given credit for accomplishing their tasks.

Superstars are simply not good team players. Why should they be, when the team is made up of incompetents doing mediocre work?

Superstars don't like sharing the spotlight. They shouldn't have to. They should be given credit for their own work. Others get credit for their own work. The leader gets credit for making it all work. See how it works?

Superstars want to look good. Let them. Don't make a superstar play "hit the ball and drag Johnny." It creates discontent and resentment and eventually puts the superstar in a position of making a choice: Do I stay and let these bozos get the credit for all my hard work, or do I go someplace else and get recognized for my talents?

If they stay, they will lose respect for the leader who is putting up with the poor performers. Eventually some superstars will lose sight of the common goal and lose faith in the process until they become mediocre or sometimes horrible employees full of resentment.

Usually at this point the leader says, "I wonder what happened." What happened was lousy leadership.

Superstars bore easily. They don't keep pace with the pack—they create their own pace, which is normally way out in front of the pack. To hold them back while Heather and Biff catch up will just irritate the superstars and slow them down.

When someone on the team slips and the rest have to pick up the slack, the leader loses credibility because she tolerates the poor performance, thus undermining the team effort even more. Typically she will then spend her efforts trying to fix the poor performer, which is a waste of time in almost all cases. This takes the leader away from doing what she should really be doing, and that is aiding the superstars in any way she can so they can get the job done.

"One bad apple can spoil the whole barrel"

An old saying that we have all heard before, understand, and agree with. But remember this as well: The whole barrel can't save the one bad apple either. Never sacrifice the barrel in favor of the one bad apple. The only way to deal with a bad apple is to throw it away.

Just like in sports: When you have a player who can't pull his weight, you trade him, don't renew his contract, or just cut him loose to be a free agent. However, as I have said before, there will always be bad employees. You can't get rid of them all. Just do the best you can to clear the path for the superstars.

"Good sales cover up a multitude of sins"

My mom and dad told me that the whole time I was growing up. They both worked in retail and knew the importance of good results. However, that's not just a line about selling—that is a line about life. It is a reminder to look at results.

While this great little saying has broad-ranging significance in several areas, it is especially important when speaking of superstars.

Many years ago as an account executive (a ten-dollar word for a salesperson) at Southwestern Bell, I was required to do many sales forecasts and reports, plus quarterly and yearly projections. I hated doing them. I didn't much believe in them and figured out very quickly that they were not really used to forecast revenue for the corporation but instead were just useless piles of paper that ended up in file drawers and were used mostly to justify someone's job, which was to generate paper. I was a good salesperson—one of the best. Always over quota. Therefore, I decided after a couple of times doing the paperwork that I would just stop. It didn't make sense to me, and I have always hated doing stuff that doesn't make sense. My boss talked to me long and hard about it. I told him I was about 200 percent of quota and I figured I was hired to sell stuff and not to do paperwork. I was just going to continue selling and they could put up with the money I was making for them and learn to live without the paperwork. He was a smart boss. He agreed. So he helped get my paperwork done for me. He knew I was right. Besides, having a salesperson that far above quota only made the boss look better.

The lesson? Superstars make their own rules.

Don't like it? Not fair? If you think that, then you obviously aren't a superstar. Superstars aren't interested in fair when it comes to protecting those who don't perform. Superstars care about results.

Superstars can write their own rules because they have the results. They don't have to live by the same rules as the mediocre, because they don't give mediocre results. That means they get to do pretty much what they damn well please—at least as long as they have outstanding results.

When the results change, then the rules change. If a superstar's results start to slip, then it's back to playing by everyone else's rules.

If you work for me and sell three times what everyone else sells, then come in when you want and stay as long as you want. I don't know what you are doing and I don't care . . . as long as it's legal and ethical, it's fine with me. I just want you to keep on doing it. Just tell me how I can help you do it. Or tell me to butt out. That'll work too.

If you are barely making quota, then your butt better be in your chair early, you should probably skip lunch, and you should let me leave before you every day so I'll at least think you are trying. You should let me know every move you are making, because your track record says you aren't making too many good moves. See why you are a problem for me? I have to be involved in all you do because you aren't a superstar. Is there any wonder why I play favorites?

We all live by different rules based on our results. I've already said that there is no reason to ever cut anyone slack. You earn slack. Great results earn you that slack.

However, that idea won't work when we have a team and when a group of people is responsible for the result. Team members all have to be treated alike. How boring. How unproductive. How stupid.

Beware the team player

You often hear people talk about how they are "team players." They brag about how it doesn't matter who gets the credit as long as the work gets done. They smile and say they have the ability to get along with everyone. People love them. They espouse all of these admirable qualities that at first glance seem to be very positive. How can things that sound so good turn out to be so bad?

The person who doesn't care who gets the credit is a person who has never gotten the credit because her own contribution has never been worthy of the credit. Once you have gotten the credit for your own outstanding performance, you would never say it doesn't matter. It always matters.

And anyone who says he can get along with everyone has the moral fiber of a wet rag. If you can get along with everyone and everyone loves you, then you don't stand for much. A person who stands his ground for his principles and won't compromise his integrity is not loved by everyone. He may be respected, but he isn't liked. What kind of person can get along with everyone? A person who can't see or is willing to tolerate the stupidity of others. A person who doesn't care that her coworkers aren't working. I don't want that person on my "team." I want people who are in touch with their beliefs, willing to fight for them, won't compromise, and won't tolerate mediocrity in themselves or others.

Don't misunderstand me here. Every person must be able to get along with others to the degree that's necessary to get the work done. Getting the work done is paramount. But working with others to accomplish the job is different from being a "team player."

Larry's short list on (not) working together:

- *Teamwork doesn't work because someone on the team won't work.*
- *Instead of teams we should create groups of superstars, exploiting their individuality.*
- *Superstars don't like to share the spotlight. Don't ask them to.*
- *Superstars love working with other superstars to achieve a common goal.*
- *The same rules don't apply to everyone. Great results earn you slack.*
- *Good sales cover up a multitude of sins.*
- *Beware the self-professed team player.*

CHAPTER 14

You gotta serve somebody

Every single person on the planet is rewarded for one thing and one thing only, and that is for serving other people. The more you serve others, the higher your reward.

In business you are rewarded for serving the customer. Where does that leave us now? Yep, that tired old worn-out topic: Customer Service.

Why are we still talking about this?

Seriously. Why? I am sick of talking about it and sick of hearing about it. Speakers speak about it, trainers train about it, writers write about it, companies promise it, and employees pretend to deliver it. The subject is beaten to death worldwide on a daily basis and yet *nothing* seems to work. The customer service that you and I get still sucks. Let me make this clear: Customer service is *not* that hard. In fact, it is so simple that it seems beyond stupid to be talking about it at all.

This is all it takes: Do what you say you are going to do when you say you are going to do it in the way you said you were going to do it. That's it. Oh yeah, and be nice about it. Now, that's it.

> ***Do what you say you are going to do***
> ***when you say you are going to do it***
> ***in the way you said you were going to do it.***

Am I asking too much?

If you make me a promise, keep it. If you give me your word, don't go back on it. If you say you are going to be there, be there—and be there when you said you would be there. If you mess up, admit it and accept the consequences. And if I am giving you money for a product or service, be at least a little grateful and friendly to me.

Is that so hard? Well, it must be, because few do it. In fact, most companies live by this credo: We're not happy until you're not happy!

So what's the problem, Larry?

Complacency. We are so used to receiving bad service that bad service has become the norm. Most people just put up with it rather than bother to complain about it. We know that if we complain, the service will either get worse or the people we are complaining to or about will just ignore us or, even worse, laugh in our faces. We eat a lousy $35 steak because we are afraid that if we send it back, the waiter will spit on it when he brings out the next one. We shy away from confrontation because we don't want the frustration of dealing with people who couldn't care less what we think.

So what's the solution?

Remember the movie *Network*? Peter Finch won an Oscar (even though he was dead) for his famous line "I'm mad as hell and I'm not going to take it anymore!" That's the solution. Refuse to take it. Just stop putting up with it.

I refuse to accept bad service. I won't let an employee or a company lie to me. I won't allow you to be rude to me. I won't let you take my money unless you have earned it. I will remind you of your promises, your advertising, and your commitments and I will expect you to honor them. I will be your worst nightmare. I will make you rue the day you lied to me. I will make you hate yourself for not living up to your word. I will rag on you until you are genuinely sorry for screwing up my order instead of just *saying* you are sorry.

Buyer beware?
I don't think so!

We all have heard that old saying "Buyer beware." We let companies mistreat us, lie to us, and cheat us, and we take it. We shrug our shoulders, roll our eyes, and deep in our subconscious minds we tell ourselves, "Buyer beware." This has to stop. When someone gives you bad service, speak up. Tell everyone not to do business with that person or that company. I believe that we should start to do business by the credo "Seller beware!"

Treat me badly and live with the consequences of your bad behavior by having me tell everyone exactly what kind of service you deliver.

Will that fix things?

Probably not; at least not at first. And certainly not if I am the only one doing it. But my complaining just might make the company or individual think twice about the service they give the next guy. My behavior won't make *my* experience any better, but it just might make his experience better. And if lots and lots and lots of people complain, then maybe service really will improve. Eventually.

But I can promise you this: Service will *never* get better if we smile, grit our teeth, and take it.

But please remember this: You don't have to be an ass about it. There is no need to cuss or be rude about it. And there is never a reason to belittle anyone on a personal level. Besides, you lose your power if you cuss or scream, and you don't want to give up your power when complaining.

However, you owe it to the company and the individual to firmly and politely point out that their service sucks, and why. The fact that you paid for the service gives you the right to complain about it. Like the time I pointed out to my mail carrier that she was leaving all of my outgoing mail behind every day. She told me that she was paid to deliver the mail, not to pick it up. I pointed out that the Priority Mail envelopes I was paying almost four bucks each to mail still had POSTAL SERVICE printed on the side, and I expected some service out of the deal. I pointed out that I wanted her, as my mail carrier, to carry the mail both ways—in *and* out of my business. She griped some more about it and I did the next appropriate thing: I called her boss.

Never hesitate to kick your complaint up the ladder. It is a waste of breath to complain to the person who has just delivered the bad service if he shows no concern about his bad service. It does no good to gripe to some minimum-wage clerk about corporate policy. Ask for the manager. Contact the corporate headquarters. Bump it up the chain of command until you reach the top and are satisfied.

And remember this: *Everyone* has a boss. Seriously. If you aren't satisfied with the answer you get, then stick with it. Don't stop until you are satisfied. Keep going up the ladder until you have had your say.

You should also document your complaint. Have specific times, places, names, invoice numbers, and receipts—every bit of proof you can come up with. This gives your complaint some teeth.

Things may not change, but you will feel better. And if they get enough people complaining about their bad service, things just might, maybe, possibly get better—though probably not.

Caution!

If you complain, you will be become known as an asshole. Believe me, I know about this one firsthand. I am known as an asshole. Doesn't really seem fair to me. I ask people to live up to their word, do what they promised me they would do, show up on time. They don't, and when I point it out to them, I am considered an asshole. That confuses me. However, I am willing to put up with my reputation. In fact, I even enjoy it a bit. Besides, is it really so bad being known as the guy who speaks up against abuse?

"Abuse? Isn't that a little extreme?"

I see it as abuse. To let a company, restaurant, hotel, airline, or employee run over you and take advantage of you and your money is abuse. I won't stand for it. When I am paying people, I refuse to let them abuse me, take advantage of me, treat me poorly, talk down to me, be late, or be rude. If that makes me an asshole, then I proudly wear the tag.

For the company (also known as the defendant):

Here is a word for those who end up listening to the few of us with the cojones to complain about bad service: Say, "Thank you." That's right. Be grateful that someone took the time to point out that you and your company have a problem. Then admit you are wrong. Yep, just suck it up and admit that you screwed up. Don't pass the buck. Admit your mistake. Don't blame another employee or another department. I don't care who screwed up. I just want someone to apologize and take responsibility and fix my problem. So say you are sorry and do your best to make me happy. If you do, there is a very good chance I will stop being your worst nightmare and instead become your best friend.

Got a problem with that? In case you do, let me remind you of something. You work for me. Sorry, but it's true. I have the money. I am *revenue*. You are *expense*. Most employees don't even know what that means. But when I am revenue, it is my money that keeps you in business, and that makes me the boss.

My money keeps your doors open and pays your salary. Be nice to me. Tell me the truth. Be there when you said you would be there. Smile at me. Say thank you. Be courteous. Kiss my butt a little bit, just like you do when the company president is talking to you. Remember this: You *need* me. Like it or not, like *me* or not, you and your company *need* me and my money. Desperately.

No customer needs a company who consistently delivers

bad service. No customer will continue to share her money with a company that employs people who aren't nice to her.

Your company can easily survive and probably even flourish without you. After all, you are just an expense. And yes, I said *just* an expense. Someone else can easily provide what you provide the company. Your services aren't that special. You aren't the only one who can do it, so get a grip on your importance. On the other hand, your company can't last without me or other people like me. No company needs an employee who upsets customers and provides bad service. Yet every company needs customers who are willing to put up with your sorry service and still spend money with them.

And keep your ego in check. Not even the world's best, most unique product being offered at a giveaway price can survive poor customer service. Consumers will gladly pay more for less when they have the confidence that they will be served well in the process.

The economic indicator

The economic condition of a company is normally a reflection of the kind of service it provides. The companies that do well in a sagging economy are the ones that provide the best service. The companies that get in trouble are the ones that provide lousy service. So serve me well, and your company will do better. Serve me well as an individual, and you will become critical to the organization you work for. Job security has a direct tie to serving the customer well. Practice it, and your chances of staying employed go way up. Don't practice it, and I personally will do my best to make sure that you work somewhere other than where I shop.

> *"There is only one boss. The customer. And he can fire every-*
> *body in the company from the chairman on down simply by*
> *spending his money somewhere else."*
>
> —SAM WALTON, founder of Wal-Mart

The real key to customer service is: A deal is a deal

You made a deal when you went into business. You agreed to provide a product or service. The deal was struck when I agreed to pay for it. At that moment, you went to work for me, which means you need to treat me well and keep your word and do everything within your power to make me happy, because it's my money, and giving it to you makes me your boss. *That* is the deal. Don't like it? Get out of business. Or don't bother getting out, that's okay, you will be gone soon enough.

Cheeseburger—cheeseburger—no Pepsi!

I love cheeseburgers. I know about cheeseburgers. I know what they look like, taste like, and smell like. I know that the best ones have grease on top of the bun and onions fried inside the meat. I know they aren't good for you, and I just don't care. You are going to die of something, and in my opinion, it might as well be with a good greasy cheeseburger in your hand.

Consequently I am always on the lookout for a good cheeseburger. When you travel as much as I do, you get the chance to sample some great ones. I even like many fast food cheeseburgers. One of my favorites comes from Sonic Drive-In. Many of you will not have had the chance to eat one of their great cheeseburgers, as they are not in every state yet. But they are in about half of the states, so many of you will know just how amazing their cheeseburger is. Sonic is based in Oklahoma City, Oklahoma, and has been around since I was in high school. They got their start in rural Oklahoma, which is where I grew up, and in my opinion is still the best place to find authentic, greasy, mouthwatering, gut-busting cheeseburgers.

One day I was in the mood for a Sonic cheeseburger. I pulled into a Sonic Drive-In, rolled down my window, and pushed the button to order my cheeseburger. That day they featured a special. It was a black plastic squeeze bottle with hot pink writing all over it and a hot pink straw sticking out of the bottle. It cost only thirty-five cents more than the large drink and you got to keep it *forever*. I had to have it. I am prone to compulsive purchases, and it was calling to me! Just as I was about to order my cheeseburger and the black plastic squeeze bottle with the hot pink writing and the hot pink straw, I noticed there was a problem. The problem was, the squeeze bottle was a Pepsi-Cola promotion. I don't like Pepsi. Sorry, Pepsi, I like some of your other products, but I am a Coke guy through and through. The sign promoting the special was very clear: The squeeze bottle was a Pepsi promotion and only came full of Pepsi.

I had to make a decision: Could I choke down a Pepsi in order to get the black plastic squeeze bottle? I decided that I could. So I pushed the button and told the guy on the other end of the line that I wanted a cheeseburger and the black plastic squeeze bottle with the hot pink writing. He said, "Sir, what would you like in that?" That was an interesting response. The sign clearly said it was a Pepsi promotion and the bottle only came full of Pepsi. It even had Pepsi written on the side in hot pink. So I said to him, "You mean I get a choice?" He said, "Sir, this is America! You *always* get a choice." I said, "Then give me a Dr Pepper."

I learned more in that ten-second exchange about customer service than I could have by reading all the books written about it, listening to all the speakers talk about it, or attending all the training sessions about how to give it. I was simply reminded, "You *always* get a choice."

My choice is to spend my money where it is appreciated. That should be your choice as well.

Sadly, there aren't really very many good stories like that about customer service. Customer service sucks. When I go into restaurants these days, if the food even shows up, I have a party.

Customer service is bad and we all know it. But beyond bad

service is this: Things just don't make sense. Policies are created that are so absurd, you would think the decision makers at some of the companies were on crack when they wrote them.

I want things to make sense!

Dallas, Texas. It's around ten p.m., and I'm checking in at the front desk of a major hotel. I am not going to tell you the name of the hotel right now, but I will tell you that two trees were involved. And in case you don't know or have forgotten, I'll also remind you that this particular hotel is famous for giving a warm chocolate-chip cookie to each customer as they check in.

As I check in at the front desk, there is another customer standing in line next to me also checking in with another clerk. When the front desk clerk hands me my cookie, I smell it and smile and can't wait to get to my room and chow down. But as the other front desk clerk hands the other customer his cookie, he declines, saying he doesn't like chocolate. (What kind of person doesn't like chocolate?) I immediately speak up and offer to take his cookie. The clerk says she can't give me the cookie because it is one cookie per guest. I say, "But he doesn't want it." The other guest says, "Yeah, I don't want it, just give it to him." She then explains she can't give me the cookie, as it was originally intended for another guest and I already have the cookie assigned to my room. I ask if their cookies really have room assignments. She doesn't think I am funny. I run into that a lot. The other guest then says, "Okay, just hand it to me and I'll hand it to him." She says it is too late for that, too, as the cookie had already been declined.

Are you frustrated just reading the story? (Doesn't it make you want to eat a chocolate-chip cookie?) This scenario doesn't make sense to me. But you have had experiences very similar to it, haven't you? Sure you have. You have stood in front of employees shaking your head in disbelief over the stupidity of the situation just as I have. The difference is, I give speeches and write books about my experiences. And I complain to the people and the companies that give me the bad service. I make my dissatisfaction known, hopefully saving the next person from the experience.

Here is the saddest thing about my cookie story. It has been ten years since I didn't get that chocolate-chip cookie, and I'm still mad about it. Okay, I'll admit that I should be over it by now. And I am over it. Almost. But the point is, I still remember every detail of the event. And I think of it every time I check into a Doubletree Hotel. More than that, hundreds of thousands of people now know this story and just might remember it next time they check into a Doubletree Hotel. Was it really worth it to the hotel chain to have me tell this story all for the price of a chocolate-chip cookie? I doubt it.

The defense for this story is that you can't control what every employee does at every moment. That's right. There is no way to know what every employee is going to do or say in every situation. But in my story, you have a front desk clerk making decisions about how a customer feels about Doubletree Hotels, and she is making that decision based on policy and procedure instead of what makes sense. That can be addressed to improve the odds of employees seeing the big picture.

Most businesses don't teach their employees to see the big picture and what might occur long-term as a result of their actions. The hotel clerk had no idea she was refusing to give a cookie to a professional speaker who stands in front of a couple hundred thousand people per year and who writes books read by that many more people. She had no idea that ten years later I was going to tell that story in this book. But if she had known all of that, I doubt it would have changed her actions. She didn't see the big picture. And she wasn't trained to just "do what makes sense"; she was trained to follow procedure.

Too many businesses today get by with doing things that just don't make sense. Things that irritate the customer and alienate employees by making them the brunt of complaints. Things that are just flat-out stupid.

I love stories like this, so here are a few more:

The union wins and the customer loses

When I speak at conventions, I normally autograph my books and I also offer my DVDs, CDs, T-shirts, and other stuff. Recently I was speaking in Las Vegas. When I had the boxes of books and other products delivered to the ballroom, I was told that the bellman couldn't enter the ballroom because it was under the jurisdiction of the decorators' union, and bellmen couldn't go in to actually deliver the boxes to the tables where they needed to be set up. I was incredulous. When I asked what

I was supposed to do, the bellman replied that he could leave them outside the room and I could carry them inside myself. That was the only option. I asked if it was hotel policy to just let the customer carry his own boxes. He said the hotel had nothing to do with it and couldn't stop it because the union made the rules. So my manager and I carried the boxes into the ballroom. The hotel, of which I am a customer, is not allowed to serve me because a union rule is in the way. The hotel suffers, the bellman suffered, as he would have gotten a bigger tip had he gone all the way into the ballroom and helped stack the boxes on the tables, and I suffered. But the union thinks they won. Is there any logic here?

The accidental terrorist

I was taking a flight from Phoenix to Tampa with a change of aircraft in Dallas. On the first leg of my flight I was served breakfast. I decided to keep the little plastic knife that I'd been given to spread cream cheese on my bagel to use when I arrived in Tampa to open the boxes of books that had been shipped there for my speech. I put the plastic knife in my inside jacket pocket for safekeeping. At the Dallas airport, the security staff singled me out to be searched as a security risk. I just have that look that makes them say, "I want to go through his stuff." In fact, I am thinking of changing my name to Random, because when they announce a random search, it always means me. As I was being searched, they discovered the plastic knife that I had slipped into my pocket during my flight. At that point, they brought in the airport police and head of security because I was attempting to transport a knife on board an airplane—a knife the airline had just given me. When I pointed out the absurdity of the situation, I reminded them that I was about to board a plane that was also a food flight, and they were going to give me another knife just like the one I was carrying. They still gave me a warning and kept the little plastic knife. Things like that bother me. Why? Because they don't make sense.

Bargain towels

I have a routine that I go through when I check into any hotel. I do it the same way every single time; that's why it's called a routine. The first thing I do when I get to my room is grab the remote control. It's a guy thing. I am convinced that women are superior to men in just about every single way except for the thumb action on a remote control! Next, I have discovered that people steal lightbulbs from hotel rooms. Trust me, they do. Rooms are cleaned during the day when the drapes are open and the natural light is coming in, so the maids don't always check the lamps. So when you check into a room, you'd better turn on the lamps or you might leave, come back, and find yourself in the dark. Third, I like good towels, so I always go into the hotel bathroom and look at the towels.

One day I checked into a hotel and upon walking into my room I grabbed the remote control. It had fifty-eight buttons; I knew this was going to be a good stay. I turned on the lights and they all came on. Then I walked into the bathroom only to see a little sign that said PLEASE DO NOT STEAL OUR TOWELS. IF YOU DO, YOU WILL BE BILLED $5 FOR EACH ONE YOU TAKE. This sign insulted me. I had never even thought of stealing their towels . . . until then. I reached up and pulled a towel down from the shelf. This was a towel! It was taller than I was, it was wide, and it was big, thick, fluffy, and soft. And it was only five dollars! I have been shopping before, and I know that this is at least a twenty-dollar towel. I left a note saying, "I'm taking four of your towels, bill me $20! Thanks!"

Good story, huh? I tell that story in my speeches. People love it because it represents how absurd signs can be and how some things just don't make sense. Early on when I told that story in my speeches, I used to say the name of the hotel where it occurred: The Harvey Hotel, Dallas, Texas. But then a guy at a speech I was doing in San Francisco heard that story and called his sister, who just happened to be the sales manager at that very Harvey Hotel in Dallas, and related my story to her. She then took the initiative to call me at my office, saying that she had heard I had stayed at her hotel and had a bad experience that I was talking about in my speeches, and she wanted to do whatever it took to make me happy so I wouldn't say bad things about her hotel in my speech. I laughed and told her that I had a wonderful experience at her hotel and got a great buy on towels while there. I then told her the entire story just as I tell it from the stage. She laughed and said that she could see my point about their sign and that they certainly didn't want all of their guests "buying" their towels for only $5 each, so they would change the sign. I told her that the story was too good to give up, but I wouldn't advertise their great towel pricing any longer and would drop the name of the hotel from the story. A few days later in the mail I received a box with four brand-new Harvey Hotel towels.

What makes my towel story different from my other stories? First of all, someone took the time to reach out to find out whether or not there was a problem. Second, she listened and was willing to see the big picture and take action to correct the issue. Third, she had a sense of humor about the whole thing. Fourth, she went the extra mile by sending me the towels both as a funny gag and as a reminder that Harvey Hotel cares enough to make things right by going beyond what is called for to make a customer happy.

My all-time favorite customer service story:

I was walking through the mall one day when I realized I needed to stop and buy some batteries. I saw a store in the mall I knew sold batteries, so I headed toward it. Again, I will not tell you the name of the store, but I will tell you that evidently their first product was a radio and they'd started in a shack somewhere. (I love getting even.)

I pulled the batteries off the rack and laid the batteries on the counter along with my cash. A guy on the other side of the counter looked at me and said, "Can I have your name, address, and telephone number?" Have you ever had that happen? Of course you have. I said, "No." Want to start having some fun in life? Then just get good at saying no. Stores don't have any idea what to do when the customer just politely says no.

In fact, if you want to have a good time, go through the drive-in lane at McDonald's. When you get to that first window, you will reach out and hand them your money and they will reach out and hand you your change. Then the clerk will say, "If you will just pull up to our second window, we'll hand your food out to you." At that point just say, "No, I think I'll just wait right here." You will screw up two hundred Happy Meals. And it will be worth it.

So the guy at the counter said to me, "Sir, we have to have your name, address, and telephone number in order to sell you the batteries." I asked him why. He then went on to tell me the number-one thing that no customer ever wants to hear. He said, "Sir, because that is our company policy." I told him I had a "customer policy" and that my customer policy was that for $1.79 worth of batteries, when I was paying cash, I didn't need to tell him who I was.

At that point, he pushed the batteries across the counter and said he wouldn't be able to sell me the batteries. I asked if there was a manager there. He told me the manager was in the back, but he would go get him. He then went in the back and came out with what I recognized right off to be a manager: It was a kid about nineteen years old. You've seen this guy, haven't you?

The manager approached the counter with his finger pointed at me, stopped in front of me with that finger about a foot from my nose, and said, "Sir, do you have a problem?"

I told him I didn't have any problem at all. He had batteries and I had money, and in America, we call that . . . a deal. He said, "You are going to have to give us your name, address, and telephone number or we are not going to sell you the batteries." I explained it just wasn't going to happen. I knew he had a company policy, but I had a customer policy. Besides, I told him that I wanted him, as the manager, to explain to me why it was necessary to give all of my personal information when I was paying cash. He then told me the second thing no customer ever wants to hear: "Because that's the way we've always done it."

I told him that I had really good news for him, because on that day, he was going to get to find a way to do it differently.

At that point, he pushed the batteries across the counter at me and said, "We aren't doing business with you!" and turned to walk away. I said, "Listen, you are the manager and I am the customer. You should be able to figure out some way for me to get the product that I came in here for and, believe it or not, am still willing to pay for, so don't walk away until you at least stop and think about this for a minute."

He stopped, thought for a while, turned, and walked by over to his computer, where he started to type. In just a minute, he took my money and handed me some change. Then he put the batteries in a bag along with a receipt that he pulled from his computer, saying to me, "There you go, I figured it out."

I asked him what he had figured out. He told me that he had just put his own name, address, and telephone number on my receipt. Not a brain surgeon, huh? At this point, he had an unhappy customer walking out the front door of his business, but now I had his name, his address, and his telephone number.

Sad? I think it's pitiful.

Why? Because he was doing exactly what he had been trained to do. He didn't have the big picture. But neither did his company. Their policy was ridiculous, didn't serve the customer, and on top of it all, didn't make any sense.

I call that my most famous story because I have told it from the stage to a couple of million people. When you consider the number of audiotapes, compact discs, videotapes, and DVDs I have sold that included that story, the number goes up by several million more people. People love that story because they have had the same experience with that store.

After about twelve years of telling that story, I received a call at my office one day from an executive with the company. He said to me, "You are probably wondering why I'm calling." I responded to him with "Actually, I've got a pretty good idea!"

He then told me that since they first started in business they had always made it their policy to collect name, address, and telephone number. But that policy was also their number-one customer complaint. I told him I would call that a clue! He went on to say that he wanted to play my video so that his store managers could hear me tell that story. I asked if there was any money involved. Seemed like a fair question. He told me there was no money involved. I told him that he could play the tape as long as they agreed to make a change. He told me they had to change; I had told too many people.

As a result, a couple of years ago, they did stop taking names, addresses, and telephone numbers, because it no longer served their customer well.

Can one person really make a difference? Of course he can. One person confronted with something that doesn't make sense who decides to stop taking it and start speaking up can indeed make a difference in the way the whole country shops.

Examine your policies and practices to make sure that they

pass the commonsense test. Ask your customers how they feel about the way you do business. Listen to your employees when they complain about certain procedures to see if there is a faster, easier, or cheaper way of doing it. Ask your employees what upsets your customers more than anything else, and then change it to serve your customer.

Beware of terms like *company policy* and *industry standard*. Stop saying things like "That's the way we have always done it." Be careful when telling a customer that you can't do something, when what you really mean is you won't do something.

I have worked with companies around the world that spend millions and millions of dollars on advertising. Some of those companies have huge television and print campaigns that brag about their products, their pricing, and their amazing customer service. Yet sometimes in business we forget that the best advertising in the whole world is a satisfied customer with a big mouth. And the worst advertising in the whole world is a dissatisfied customer with a big mouth.

As a leader, don't let your employees get so caught up in the process of doing business that they forget why they are there: to serve customers. Remember and remind others that we all do what we do for only one reason and that is to serve others, knowing that the better we serve others, the better we are in turn served. That's why we work: to serve others. How we serve others is only a process that must be susceptible to the circumstances of the moment.

We all do what we do for one reason and one reason only, and that is to serve others, knowing that the better we serve others, the better we are in turn served.

"I'm confused about ethics now, Larry!"

"You are all about right and wrong and doing what is ethical. You say to do exactly what your company tells you to do. What about the guy in your Sonic story who was supposed to give you a Pepsi and yet gave you a Dr Pepper? Wasn't that a violation of ethics? Didn't he break the rules just to make you happy?

"In your RadioShack story, the clerk was supposed to get your name, address, and telephone number. He was only doing his job. If he didn't get that information, wouldn't that have been wrong?

"At Doubletree Hotel, you really weren't supposed to get a second cookie. Why is the employee wrong for doing what she was told to do?"

You are right! I put these employees in a position of choosing between corporate policy and serving the customer well. I caused an ethical dilemma. Good for me. Corporations must decide what's really important and allow their employees some latitude in making that happen. It's a true shame that an employee is made to go against policy just to provide good service. The answer to every ethical question should be based on whether it's legal and moral, makes sense, and is the right thing to do to serve the customer well.

"Do you ever get any good service, Larry?"

Sure I do. In fact, I actually believe that there is more good service being delivered every day than there is bad service. However, I am like almost everyone who shops and spends money: I don't remember the good service—at least, not for very long. And I don't talk about it much. Oh sure, I'll mention it for a day or two to the people who enjoyed the good service with me, and I might even tell someone who plans on spending their money at a certain place about my last experience there if it was a good one. But the good memories slip away pretty quickly. That is just the way it works with good service. We all forget. Bad service doesn't work that way. We all remember bad service and we tell everyone we know about it. With bad service, you never forget. What's the lesson for those of us providing service? Do everything within your power to make sure the service we provide isn't bad, so the customer won't have anything to remember or talk about.

There is such a thing as a bad customer

As you can tell, I am about as pro-customer as you can possibly get. However, sometimes you will run into a customer who just isn't worth it. The profit you make just isn't going to be worth the abuse you will have to take to earn it.

If the customer is abusive to an employee on a personal level, that is a customer who just isn't worth having. Which is different from "if the customer gets mad because you have done something wrong." Customers have the right to get mad when a mistake has been made. They may even have the right to scream and yell, depending on your reaction to their complaint. But they never have the right to become personally abusive.

Some customers are just mean. Stop and ask yourself if their business is worth it. If it is, suck it up and take it and choose to deal with their abuse. However, if it isn't worth it, walk away and don't look back.

Some customers will constantly beat you up over your price. They don't care about the relationship or your service; they just want the best price. They threaten you with your competitors and with leaving you. Is this customer worth having? Remember what my friend Mark Sanborn, author of *The Fred Factor*, says: "The customers who are willing to pay you the least will always demand the most."

In these cases, I suggest you have a conversation with your customers explaining that you won't be accepting their business any longer, and tell them exactly why. You might be surprised by their response. They may honestly have no idea they are being hard to get along with. If that is the case, explain it to them and give them another chance if they ask for one. However, if they become indignant and ticked off, just ask them nicely to take their business elsewhere.

Larry's short list for serving others well:

- *We are rewarded in life for only one thing: serving others well.*
- *Unfortunately, bad service has become the norm.*
- *Complain to the appropriate person about poor service.*
- *If you receive a complaint, admit your responsibility, apologize, and fix the problem.*
- *Policies and procedures should at least pass the commonsense test.*
- *Just one person can certainly make a difference in the way the whole world shops.*
- *The better we serve others, the better we are in turn served.*

CHAPTER 15

Nothing happens until something is sold

Want to lose weight? It's simple. You may argue that point and try to complicate it all you want, but there are only two simple ways to lose weight: Eat less and exercise more. You can buy every diet book, diet pill, diet shake, diet bar, and diet meal and join every diet society in the world and none of it will help you lose a pound permanently. It isn't until you understand that the only way to lose weight permanently and healthfully is to take in fewer calories and burn more calories. Two simple things that are guaranteed to work every single time. No one can argue it—no doctor can dispute it. Two simple ideas that always work.

It's just about that easy in business, too. There are only two ways to be more profitable in business: Reduce expenses or increase income. It doesn't get more complicated than that. And no one can dispute these two things either. Again, two simple ideas that always work. And there are lots of ways to do both of those things.

You can do many things to reduce expenses. I think the best way to do that is to dump all of those employees who don't work. People are your biggest expense, and that's the most effective place to start for sure. Then you can look at the other things. But that is not my area of expertise.

I have never been good at cutting back on expenses. I don't like to shop for bargains and I don't like to buy or own anything less than the best. I don't like living on less of anything, personally or professionally. Because I was never good at living with less, I have spent my life trying to figure out how to get more. That's what I am good at: increasing income. Figuring out how to earn more so I can have the best of everything is my area of expertise.

The easiest way I know of to increase income is to sell. I'm a salesman. I always have been and I always will be. I grew up selling. I dragged tomatoes around in a little red wagon and sold them door-to-door before I was even in school. I was good at it. I always had money in my pocket. My family didn't have much, but even as a kid I always had a little change. I would do whatever it took to have money. I picked up pop bottles along the highway and sold them for two cents apiece. I trimmed trees for $1.50 per tree—not one of my best negotiations, I must admit. When the tree is six feet tall it isn't bad; when the tree is forty feet tall, it's a different story! I sold candy bars and greeting cards and the *Grit* newspaper—remember *Grit*?

Because my parents both worked in retail, I grew up around people who sold to make a living. My grandfather was a "carny," who sold pony rides and tickets to see his monkey and his bear.

When he quit the carnival, he bought and sold pigs and cattle. From the time I could barely walk, I heard him haggle back and forth, ask for the sale, and collect the money.

My transition to a professional salesman was a natural one. I sold telephones for a living at Southwestern Bell and later at my own company. I have spent the last seventeen years selling speeches. Along with the speeches came the books, tapes, videos, DVDs and CDs, T-shirts, coffee mugs, shot glasses, bobble heads, and every other bit of paraphernalia that I could come up with to exploit my speaking and to put a buck in my pocket. And I am a master at it. Most speakers show up with a little table and a few books or tapes. When I show up, it looks like a rock concert. I am the Gene Simmons/KISS of professional speaking; if I can put my name and slogan on it, I'll do it and sell it.

I am always amazed that people in the speaking business say they are in the speaking business and yet never get into the business of speaking. There is a difference. I am in the business of speaking. But I am primarily in the business of self-promotion. I am my biggest product. I am a business. And one of the things I know about my business is this: My product must be sold. It doesn't matter how good I am or how amazing my speech or book is, it must be sold. The same goes for you. I don't care how good you are, how good your product is, what your reputation is, how much credibility you have, how well priced you are, or what your competitive advantages are; none of it matters. In the end, your product must be sold.

Don't buy it? Think about this: Every movie you see has been sold. Why do you think George Clooney shows up on *Letterman*? It's not just to shoot the breeze—it's to sell you on going to his upcoming movie. Why do authors show up on the *Today* show and *Good Morning America*? Do you think it's because Matt or Diane are really interested in what those authors have to say? Sorry, the publisher and author want to sell you the book. Why is that billboard there on the highway? To sell you. It's always about selling. That's why every thirty-minute television show is only twenty-one minutes long. They have to make time for nine minutes of selling in order to pay for the twenty-one minutes of programming.

You, your product, and your business must all be sold. If no one is selling, then no one is buying and you can't last long. The old saying "Build a better mousetrap and the world will beat a path to your door" is total crap. No one is going to beat a path to your door for much of anything, especially not a mousetrap! Everything must be sold.

Bad Selling vs. Good Selling

I entered the business of speaking as a sales trainer. At one time I wrote sales training manuals while employed at the Bell System, and I knew how to sell. So it was a natural thing for me to become a sales trainer.

I went to the annual meetings of the National Speakers Association, where I would go to the sessions taught by and attended by the best sales trainers on the planet. I would listen to them discuss the future of sales training. I read every book I could find about selling. What I learned from all of this is that most sales trainers have made selling about techniques. It isn't about techniques—it is much bigger than that.

This is technique training: "When the customer says 'this,' then you say 'that.'" The problem? The customer never says "this" and you are stuck with all of "that." Yet this is what most sales training is based on: techniques.

I suggest that everyone throw away all sales techniques and instead learn to sell based on principles.

You serve best when you sell well.

You already know how I feel about serving the customer. I believe that selling the customer is serving the customer. When you have a product that helps customers, you owe it to customers to sell it to them. To not offer customers something that can genuinely serve them well is a lack of good service.

Why your sales results suck

The main reason salespeople don't sell is because they are lousy salespeople. They don't make enough sales calls. They don't ask the customer to buy. They don't know how to say thank you. They have no training. They don't know their product line. They don't know anything about their competition. They aren't held responsible for lousy results. They suck.

If your sales suck,
it's because as a salesperson,
you suck!

Don't oversell

You might be saying, "How can you oversell?" especially when I am the big advocate of selling yourself out of any problem. Let me explain.

I go to Danny's Family Car Wash—a local car wash chain in Scottsdale, Arizona. They do a great job at a great price. I go fairly often because I am a firm believer that how clean your car is reflects what kind of person you are. Therefore, I want a clean car both inside and out. When you pull up to the car wash, a team runs out and starts to vacuum the car, asking if you want gas, oil change, or a wax job (I usually ask for a Brazilian wax, which always confuses them). Then they send an inspector over to look at your car. He will point out dings in your windshield, which they will gladly fix for a charge. He will look at your floor mats and suggest a shampoo, which they will also do for a charge. He checks the wear on your tires and the road tar on your fender wells—you name it, he checks it. While I appreciate it, sometimes an overzealous employee will take it too far—to the point where it becomes annoying. I was recently there getting my wife's Mini Cooper washed when the inspector came over and said, "Ooooh, here's one that really needs a wax job!" I said, "Really? It's never even been washed before—it only has two hundred miles on it, how could it already really need a wax job?" He was embarrassed . . . and he should have been. He had oversold. He had pushed a service I obviously didn't need.

What's the problem with that? He destroyed his credibility

with me. I no longer felt like I was being served well; I just felt like I was being hustled. I believe people love to be sold and they hate to be hustled. Sadly, the line has become blurred due to bad salespeople who don't know the difference.

> *People love to be sold and they hate to be hustled.*

Sell with courtesy. Sell with tact. Sell with common sense. Don't push. Be sensitive. Back off when you feel you should back off. Ask for the sale when you feel it's appropriate to ask. Use your head, your ears, your brain, and your heart to serve your customers well by selling to them with courtesy.

People buy for their reasons, not yours

People will shell out the money when they have a reason to and not before. That reason has to be more than the fact that you need the sale. No customer really cares how badly the salesperson needs to make the sale. So give your customer a reason. Sometimes it doesn't even have to be a good reason. Many customers are just begging for permission to buy—your job is to give them permission by giving them a reason to buy.

About a thousand years ago, I heard a sales tape or read a book or heard in a seminar that there are only five reasons why people don't buy. They are: no need, no hurry, no money, no want, and no trust. I wish I knew who said it, as I would gladly give them credit. It has been too many years and I have heard too much stuff to sort it out at this point. These five reasons have stuck with me for many years and have helped me make many sales. If you use them and decide to give someone credit for teaching this idea to you, then you can say that you heard it from me, but rest assured it is not original.

These five reasons people don't buy are so helpful once you understand what they mean.

No need. This one is actually no big deal. People rarely buy what they really need. If they really do need it, they will buy it without your help. You won't have much involvement in the selling process because, after all, they really need it. Notice that there are no retail toilet paper salespeople.

No hurry. The customer needs it, he wants it, but there just isn't much hurry to get it. A challenge. You must create a sense of urgency. Show him the benefits of making the decision now instead of later. Prove how waiting is a bad idea. If all else fails, just ask him why he is putting off buying something he really needs and wants and is eventually going to buy anyway. You might find out that he has . . .

No money. However, that really stops very few people from buying. People routinely buy what they don't need, simply because they want it. Credit is rarely an issue. Bankruptcy . . . no problem. Bad credit . . . no problem. No job . . . no problem. Too stupid and lazy to pay your bills . . . no problem. A lack of money is just not an issue for most people. Besides, people will usually lie to you about this one. They have the money, but they just don't want you to know it! Remember that people always get in a hurry to buy and find the money to buy if they want it badly enough. Which brings us to the real biggie in the list of reasons why people don't buy:

No want. If people want something badly enough, they will move heaven and earth to get it. They will obsess, lose sleep, lie, cheat, and steal to have it. Your job as a salesperson? Make people want what you have to sell. Help them obsess—make them smell it, taste it, dream about it, and lose sleep over it. Make them want it so much, it consumes their every thought. Then just get out of the way and let them write you a check. And they will, unless there is:

No trust. If people don't trust you, then forget it. They won't share their money with people they don't trust. Look smarmy? You don't get their money. Come across as a fast-talker? No check for you. Bad reputation? I'll go elsewhere, thank you. Got it? Be the kind of person others can trust.

As I write this paragraph, I have been waiting for a salesperson to come to my home to sell me a pair of those cosmic custom wood garage doors for my house. We had an appointment at 11:00 a.m. It's now after 2:00 p.m. and he hasn't showed and hasn't called to explain why he is running late. I just called his voice mail to tell him to forget it. If a salesperson can't figure out a way to keep his appointment to sell me the product, or at least call me to let me know there is a problem, then I can't trust him with any other part of the entire transaction. Trust has been destroyed. I'll spend my money with someone else. See how it works?

Selling is simple!

Look successful

People want to buy from salespeople who are successful. Since we gather information first and primarily by sight and then form our opinions in the same way, it is important to look successful. A look of success in your office, your clothes, your briefcase, and your car are all signs that you are more than likely doing okay as a salesperson. This can be faked, I know, but not for very long.

No one wants to buy from a salesperson who drives a worn-out old beater for a car or wears clothes that are out-of-date and worn thin or wears shoes with worn-down heels. Those things are testaments to the fact that you aren't doing well, which translates into the fact that you aren't a very good salesperson. Which means that most of us don't want to buy from you.

Look great. Dress well. Drive the best car you can possibly afford to drive. And keep that car clean!

Be friendly

People like to buy from people they like being around. Be that kind of person. Sounds simple enough, doesn't it? But the fact is, most people just aren't friendly. Don't be overly friendly, though. You aren't my best buddy, so don't act like you are. Don't touch me except to shake my hand if I offer it. Don't be overly gregarious. Don't invade my space. Be professional, courteous, respectful, and friendly.

Ask

The Bible says, "Ye have not because ye ask not." The Bible is absolutely correct. You aren't selling enough because you aren't asking enough.

Ask. Ask. Ask. Ask. Ask! Many people would gladly buy if someone would just ask them. People will tell you just about anything you want to know if you will only ask. Become a master asker.

Think about the power of asking one more person to buy each day. Consider a work year of 220 days, which would give 220 additional people the opportunity to buy from you. If you were to close only 10 percent of those people, it would produce twenty-two more sales per year. How much more money would that mean to you in commission? Figure it out and see how simple it is to increase your income by simply asking one more person per day to buy from you.

The result of asking is this: They can either say yes or say no. There are derivatives of these two, but it basically comes down to either yes or no. If they say yes, write it up and take the money. If they say no, which is what people fear most, remember this: Asking is not fatal. You never die when the customer says no. Just go ahead and ask.

Ask more from your customers. Ask more from your employer. Ask more from your employees. But before you ask more from anyone else, first ask more from yourself.

Find out what people want

Find out what people want and give them more of it. Find out what they don't want and don't give them any of that. Could anything be simpler? That's really all it takes to sell more: Just find out what they want and give it to them. The problem is that we don't always know what they want. So then what? Find out.

How do you find out what people want? Again, just ask. I know . . . broken record!

Be observant

Observe the buying habits of your customers. Pay attention to what people buy, how they buy, and when they buy. Observe your competitors . . . see how the other people in your business sell. Don't copy what they do, but learn from what they are doing right and what they are doing wrong.

"All of us are watchers—of television, of time clocks, of traffic on the freeway—but few are observers. Everyone is looking; not many are seeing." —PETER M. LESCHAK, author, *Trials by Wildfire*

Listen

This is a really tough one for most people. In fact, it is the one thing that is nearly impossible for people to do. People are always telling you what they think—of you, your competitors, and your products. Listen to them. That information you have been missing is important.

Most people are horrible listeners. They think that listening is that short period of time when you are waiting for the other person to shut up so you can talk again. Wrong. Listening is paying attention. Most people don't listen unless it is something they want to hear. Say something they don't want to hear, and they'll quit listening. Try it. When you are paying at the cash register for your breakfast and the cashier says, "How was everything?" tell her. Trust me, she doesn't want to know that your eggs weren't over easy, they were over barely, and the hash browns were actually hash beige. She doesn't want to hear about the fact that you never got a refill on your coffee and it took ten minutes to get the check. She wants you to say what 99.99 percent of all previous customers said: "Fine."

Listening has become a lost art. Maybe it's because we all think that what we have to say is so important that we don't pay much attention to what anyone else has to say. It's not that they can't listen or don't know how to listen, it's that we don't care enough to choose to listen.

Circulate

"You've got to circulate to percolate."

—CAVETT ROBERT, founder, National Speakers Association

This is one where you have to be careful. You know people who open every conversation by handing out a business card and explaining what they do. I find this offensive. I don't want every encounter with a stranger to become a sales pitch. I don't want to feel like I am trapped in a Chamber of Commerce meeting.

Networking groups

Time to step on some more toes! I would steer clear of networking groups and their meetings. I know that will get some of you riled up. About half of all salespeople live and die by their networking group. Networking groups are usually just salespeople trying to sell their stuff to other salespeople. Few actually exchange worthwhile leads. I will guarantee that the very top salespeople in any industry don't waste their time going to networking meetings. They take the same amount of time and use it to stay in front of customers. A happy, satisfied customer will do more for your reputation and get you a lot more business than any little group of barely-making-it salespeople.

Unfair to networking groups? Ask everyone in your networking group where they rank among other professional salespeople in their industry. My bet is that very few, if any of them, will rank in the top 25 percent of their industry in terms of results. Ask what their average income is. If they will tell you the truth, which they won't, I'll bet that you want to make considerably more money than that.

The argument I will get on this point is: The more people who know what you do, the more those people can refer you to other people they encounter who need your services. Be careful whom you refer. Unless you have personally used someone's services and spent your own money paying them for what they do, you don't want to recommend them to anyone else. They may not have a good experience and it will come back to bite you in the butt. This will hurt your reputation. I never refer anyone to a friend unless I have personally used him for the service I am recommending, and then I still tell my friend that I had a good experience but she is on her own. I don't want anyone upset with me because I recommended someone who turned out to be a loser.

But you still have to circulate. Here's my idea on how to do it: Get involved. Get known. Go to charity events, civic events, wine tastings, art fairs, church, whatever. Be around people. Not with a handful of business cards to pass out. Don't even go with the idea of getting more business. Instead go there and get involved in the event. Be the kind of person others admire, can count on, trust, and enjoy spending time with. After you have developed that reputation, people will start to ask you what you do and you will be amazed at how many people will want to work with you. You will attract others based on your character. What an idea, huh? People will actually come to you because they want to do business with you because of who you are and what you stand for. That's how to circulate!

Sell it now

A few years ago, I went to a cigar store in Scottsdale, Arizona. At the time, I was smoking a particular Arturo Fuente cigar that had become hard to find. I was amazed when I walked in and found two boxes of my favorite little cigar on the shelf. I grabbed both the open box and the full box that was tucked in behind it and happily trotted off to the counter. The store owner told me that I could buy only four cigars, as he had put a limit on that particular cigar. I asked him why he would want to turn away a customer willing to buy his entire stock. He told me that other people might come in wanting that cigar and he wanted to make sure he had some so he could make them happy. I pointed out that other people also might *not* come in and want that cigar, which meant that he wouldn't be selling any of the cigars. He said that was okay, they would sell eventually. Is this making sense to you? It didn't to me. Here was a guy who was limiting his income for the day in hopes of making a customer who might never even show up happy. A guy who wants to make possible future customers happy, and yet is willing to make a customer with money in his hand standing right in front of him, unhappy.

I sell books, T-shirts, DVDs, and CDs and other paraphernalia at the back of the room when I speak. If I run out and still have customers standing there with money in their hands, I take their money and promise to have the product they want mailed to them the next day and I will pay the shipping. Many times they say they will just go to my Web site to buy instead. I discourage that. One of the ways I discourage it is by having higher prices on the Web site and offering the products slightly cheaper at the back of the room on the day of my program. Many people in my business don't understand why I care. The customers said they were going to buy anyway, so what difference does it really make, especially when I make more money when they buy from the Web site? Here is the reason: People buy on impulse. They have just heard me. They liked me. They want a piece of me. Tomorrow, the passion will have died a bit. They will get busy with their lives and travel and business and they just won't get around to ordering. I'll bet only 25 percent of those who say they are going to order actually go online and place the order. If I take the money out of their hands while the passion is high, I get all of the orders. And the few bucks it takes to mail it is worth it.

Did you ever go in a store, shop around, find exactly what you wanted, only to be told that the store doesn't have any in stock? You are standing in front of a brand-new one sitting there on the showroom floor, and they are telling you they don't have any. It has happened to me many times and somehow the words "We don't have any" when I am standing in front of one just don't compute in my brain. Don't tell me you don't have one when I am looking at one. The response is "But that is the floor model. We have to have it to sell other people." What about me? Don't you want to sell me? Those companies who won't sell the floor model are making a mistake. Sell what you've got. People buy on impulse; when they want it, they usually want it now. Let them have it. Never pass up a chance to make a sale right now! Get the money *now*—take the order *now*—get the contract signed *now*—get the commitment *now*. One more time . . . today, not tomorrow.

Know what you are talking about

You don't know enough. Don't argue. There is more to learn. Much more. You never stop learning about your product, your company, your competitors, or how to be a better person. Keep learning. If you don't have five great books on your desk, then you aren't keeping up. If you don't have a couple of business books, a novel, a biography, and something light for entertainment as well as a stack of magazines, then you aren't gaining any momentum. Plus, you will be boring to talk to. Read. Go to seminars. Listen to audiotapes and CDs in your car. Stay informed.

Even more you can do to sell more:

Be honest. Every time and without exception, even when it's hard. In fact, especially when it's hard. If your product won't do it, then say it won't. Never dance around an answer, never lie, and never mask it; just fess up.

Return calls. Do it promptly, not days later with some feeble excuse.

Take notes. Work from document, not from memory. Not only will it give you more information to work with, the customer will give you better information when they know you are writing it down. They want you to write down good stuff, and they will give you better information the instant you pick up the pen. If you are on the phone, tell them you are taking notes for the same result.

Be on time. Appointments are made for a reason. Keep them. They are a promise to appear just like a check is a promise to pay. Don't bounce the check on your appointment!

Be great on the telephone. We gather information by sight. On the phone you lose that ability. You have to make up for it with your voice, inflection, volume, enthusiasm, and tone. Give good verbal feedback on the phone. Let the other person know you are listening by speaking up when they say something. At the very least, grunt at them periodically so they will know you are there. And be good with the phone technically. Don't cut people off when transferring them. If you aren't smart enough to transfer my call, you aren't smart enough to sell me something.

Deliver more than you promise. Never let the customer say, "I expected more."

Follow up. The easiest customer to sell is the customer who is happy with what he just bought from you.

Shut up. It is as important to know when to shut up as it is to know when to speak up. Never keep talking just because you have more to say. It's easier to talk your way out of a sale than it is to talk your way into a sale.

Have a great handshake. Not one of those dead-fish things or grab-the-fingertip things. This seems to be more of a problem for women than men, though many times after shaking hands with a man I have had the feeling I needed to run and wash something nasty and dead off my fingers. Just grab the other person's hand and give it a good shake. No more than two or three times. Don't pump it or crush it or dead-fish it. Reach in far enough so the web between your thumb and forefinger touches the web between his thumb and forefinger, and then give it two pumps. Don't hold on to it after you are finished with the shaking. That's too personal and it invades others' space. When someone pulls me in close to speak to me, all while keeping hold of my hand, I always feel like some evangelist is trying to save my soul and get into my wallet for my money! Can you tell I've been taken before?

By the way, some people don't like to shake hands. Trump hates it. So does Howie Mandel. Here's the rule: If they offer, take it. If they don't offer, then don't push it. If you offer and they don't take it, that's okay—they might be a germophobe. Move on.

Bounce back. You can't win them all. Bad stuff happens. You won't sell the one you were just positive you were going to sell. In fact, the very sale you already spent the commission on is the one you probably won't get. It happens. You lose. Bounce back. You don't need to sell them all. You just need to sell the next one. So keep moving.

Capitalize on your success. Don't make a big sale and then rest on your laurels. (*Laurels* in this case means both your accomplishments and your big fat butt.) The best time to make the next sale is when you are high on the adrenaline of your last sale. If you feel invincible, chances are you will be.

Trashing a stupid sales idea

Remember the old ABC's of Selling? Always Be Closing. There was even a popular video used by thousands of organizations called *The ABC's of Selling*. What a stupid, horrible, bad idea. I am sure that this concept is what gave selling and salespeople a bad name. You were instructed to constantly ask for the sale. I mean constantly! Just keep closing and you will be a successful salesperson. People don't want to be closed all the time. If you begin every appointment with a closing question, and then try to close after every point you make, pretty soon your customers are going to start making less than complimentary statements about your mama.

People buy for one reason more than any other reason

They also will do business with you for one reason more than any other reason. That's right . . . one reason. Know what that reason is? Neither do I.

It's easy to find out. Again, all you have to do is ask. That's right. Just ask. Simply say, "It has been my experience that people buy for one reason more than any other reason. What will be the one reason that will cause you either to buy or not to buy?" Think their answer might be helpful?

Still afraid to ask? Then pay attention, be observant, listen . . . all that stuff I have been talking about. But don't complicate things. Find out what people want and give it to them. Again, I've said it already. People rarely believe it can really be so simple.

Want proof? Why do you go to your dry cleaner? Is it more convenient? Cheaper? Friendlier? They give you the one thing you are looking for more than any other dry cleaner. If they didn't, you would go to a different dry cleaner.

The same thing applies to your grocery store. It applies to your favorite restaurant. Bar. Gym. You name it, the places you go deliver the one thing you want in order for you to do business with them.

I bank for suckers

Before moving to Arizona, I lived in Tulsa, Oklahoma. I went to the same bank, State Bank, for several years. Want to know why I went to that bank? I don't care; I'm going to tell you anyway. Red suckers. That's right, they gave me red suckers. Is that a good reason to do business with a bank? Of course it is! I'm the customer, and I can't be wrong.

I am a drive-in bank guy. At one point I had to go inside the bank to open the account, but I don't even remember it. I just always go to the drive-in. One day I pulled into the drive-in with my two boys and my two dogs. My dogs were named Elvis and Nixon. (I have noticed that when you give your dog a name, over a period of time the dog becomes like the name. Elvis was a female English bulldog who when she died was obese and on drugs. Nixon was a German shepherd who ate an audiocassette tape. But we lost only seventeen and a half minutes of it.)

Anyway, as I sat at the window of the drive-in bank doing my various transactions, the little drawer came out with two dog biscuits in it. Cute, huh? I gave one to Elvis and one to Nixon and my dogs were happy.

The drawer then came back out with two suckers in it. I gave one to my son Tyler and the other to my son Patrick, and my boys were happy.

I looked back at the teller and tapped my chest with a questioning look on my face. She asked, "So what do *you* want?" I told her I didn't want a dog biscuit! So the drawer came back out with a sucker in it: a green sucker. No one really eats green suckers so I put it back in the drawer and sent it back in. She asked what the problem was and I told her I wanted a red sucker. (For those of you who are uninformed in the ways of suckers, red is a flavor, not just a color.) She sent out a red sucker and I was happy.

About a week later I returned to the drive-in alone. I went to the same spot, but a different teller was helping me. However, the original teller was also there, working a different window. When the original teller saw me, she turned to my teller and said, "That guy likes red suckers." So I ended up with a red sucker again. At that point, a pattern had been established. I became known as the guy who liked red suckers. Every time I went to the bank, all of the tellers knew to give me a red sucker.

About six months into this red sucker phenomenon, I pulled into the bank at five minutes after six p.m. The drive-in was closed, but I could see the employees still in there! I waved at the tellers and they all waved back at me while shaking their heads from side to side and smiling. I then drove around to the front of the bank where the ATM was located inside the foyer. As I stood at the ATM doing my transaction, I was right next to the big glass front door of the lobby where again I could see all the tellers, and again we waved at each other. As I became more involved in my transaction, I heard the mail slot in the front door come open and I saw a hand come through it, holding a red sucker.

My wife and I have separate bank accounts. She has her bank and I have mine. She asked me one day about the rates I get at my bank. I'm not sure my bank has rates. They don't need rates—they have red suckers. When my son turned eighteen and needed his own checking account, I asked him whether he was going to use my bank or my wife's. He said, "That's easy, you get suckers." So they got a new customer . . . not a very good one, but they did okay on overdraft charges.

I did business with that bank for years until I moved away, all because of one simple thing: red suckers.

Larry's short list for selling:

- *There are two simple ways for business to be more profitable: reduce expenses or increase income.*
- *Selling should be based on principles, not techniques.*
- *Selling is serving.*
- *The five reasons people won't buy: no need, no hurry, no money, no want, or no trust.*
- *To sell more:*
  - *Look successful*
  - *Be friendly*
  - *Ask*
  - *Be observant*
  - *Listen*

- Circulate
- Keep learning
- To sell even more:
    - Be honest
    - Return calls
    - Take notes
    - Be on time
    - Become great on the telephone
    - Underpromise and overdeliver
    - Follow up
    - Have a great handshake
    - Bounce back
- People buy for one main reason; find out what it is. Ask.

CHAPTER 16

Short, hard, expensive lessons

Some lessons are so short, they don't require an entire chapter or even a whole paragraph. Those lessons are usually the hardest and most expensive to learn. Hopefully, they will be the easiest for you to remember.

Short Lessons:

Do what you know is the right thing to do. And don't kid yourself; you always know the right thing to do. The right thing to do is rarely the easy thing to do.

People will usually lie to protect themselves.

Résumés are rarely accurate.

Companies and individuals overpromise and under-deliver. It is a fact of life. Knowing that will save you time, money, and disappointment.

Everything costs more than you originally thought it would.

Everything takes longer than you originally thought it would.

When someone says, "I am a people person," that means he will spend more time socializing than working.

When someone says, "I don't really like working with others," hire her and give her an office with a door and a lot of work to do and then watch it get done.

Prove you are smarter than everyone by hiring people who are smarter than you.

People are selfish. Understand it, and manage it as best you can.

Of all the people who will never leave you, you are the only one.

Never tolerate mediocrity.

Don't expect others to make you rich if you are keeping them broke.

The more successful you become, the fewer friends you will have.

Take your job seriously—not yourself.

Everyone wants you to be successful, just not more successful than they are.

When someone says they will try, bet your money it won't happen.

Stress comes from knowing what is right and doing what is wrong.

Implement now, perfect later.

If you aren't willing to put your money where your mouth is, you don't really believe in what you are doing.

There is no such thing as giving 110 percent. A hundred percent is all there is—you can't give more than all there is; that's why it's called all there is.

People will pay little attention to what you have to say. Most won't even believe what you have to say. They will, however, pay attention to see if you believe what you have to say.

Training is expensive, but stupid employees are more expensive.

People motivate themselves.

Be on time. There is never an excuse to be late.

The customers have the money. Give them what they want, and they will share it with you.

Look at the numbers, look at the facts, and then trust your gut.

Disrespect is the number-one grounds for dismissal.

Knowledge is not power; the implementation of knowledge is power.

Few people will turn to themselves to take responsibility for their results until they have exhausted all opportunities to blame someone else.

It's cheaper to fight bad employees when they are on the outside of the company.

Superstar employees will leave you no matter what you do to keep them.

It is impossible to grow without risk.

Sometimes you lose. When it happens, don't be an asshole about it.

They don't ask how, they ask how many.

Everyone does what they want to do, when they want to do it, and not until then.

The best advertisement in the whole world is a satisfied customer with a big mouth. The worst advertisement in the whole world is an unsatisfied customer with a big mouth.

Don't worry too much about making the right decision. Just make the decision, and then make the decision right.

Inspect what you expect. Stuff doesn't just happen; you have to make sure it happens.

You always need a Plan B, except when you don't have one. In that case, you have to make your only plan work.

You can sell your way out of almost any problem.

Change is inevitable, but growth is optional.

When you screw up, admit it, ask forgiveness, and get back to work.

What you resist persists.

You can't get a good deal from a bad guy.

Question everything.

Sometimes the best thing you can do is walk away.

Not all problems can be fixed.

Pay your taxes first, yourself second, and everyone else after that.

Trust, once destroyed, can never be fully regained.

If it starts to become complicated, then stop, regroup, and start over. Success is always simple.

Customers are short on tolerance and have very long memories.

Better to pay a good attorney than a bad employee.

The activity that you reward will get done.

Business is like golf; it's not so much about hitting the right shot every time, it's more about being able to correct a mishit.

Dumb it down. Don't expect others to understand what you are thinking or saying. Always make it as simple as you possibly can.

People treat you the way you teach them to treat you.

Praise in public and critique in private.

Don't expect respect if you don't show respect.

Don't let customers take advantage of you.

Everything has a price, including both success and failure. Choose either one and be prepared to the pay the price.

One more time, because it is important enough to repeat: **Do the right thing.** No matter what. Even when it is the unpopular thing. Even when it's the most expensive thing. Even when it's embarrassing. And if you have to ask if it's the right thing . . . it isn't. You never have to ask whether it's the right thing. You always know. So do it.

CHAPTER 17

Larry's dirty dozen employee handbook

1. Focus on accomplishment. Be known as the person who gets things done.

2. Develop a reputation that you are proud of.

3. Be trustworthy. Be the person who can keep a secret, isn't a gossip, and can be counted on in all situations.

4. When you give your word, keep it. Without exception.

5. Be on time. Be where you are supposed to be when you are expected to be there.

6. Don't brag. It's obnoxious and it alienates others.

7. Don't complain. No one cares, and they have problems of their own to deal with.

8. Friendship among coworkers is a bonus. It is not required or to be expected.

9. Don't tolerate abuse, disrespect, or a lack of ethics or integrity from your employer. Life is short; there are other jobs.

10. Find out what the single most important thing is about your job, and then make sure it gets done. If nothing else gets done, make sure that one thing gets done.

11. Serve the customer well whether you call the customer a client, patient, coworker, or boss. Your rewards in life are in direct proportion to the service you provide.

12. Remember that you work for someone. That person has the right to say what you do, when you do it, and how you do it.

CHAPTER **18**

Larry's dirty dozen employer handbook

1. Set high expectations for every employee. Clearly communicate those expectations. Manage to those expectations. Inspect what you expect.

2. Be decisive. Make the decision, and then make the decision right.

3. Don't concern yourself with being liked. Instead, be respected.

4. Pay people well. And then never mess with people's money.

5. Disrespect is grounds for immediate dismissal.

6. Discover your uniqueness and learn to exploit it in the service of others.

7. If it's broken, fix it fast before the problem grows and spreads.

8. Reward life skills and personal growth. Good people do a good job and bad people do a bad job.

9. A deal is a deal. Keep your word with customers and employees.

10. Fire people when they need to be fired—don't wait too long or second-guess yourself.

11. When hiring, beware of articulate incompetents who talk a good game but can't deliver.

12. Keep it simple. When it begins to feel complicated, stop, evaluate, simplify, and begin again.

CHAPTER 19

So now what?

That's actually one question I don't have the answer to.

You have read my ideas and opinions. You know what I think about how a business should be run. I've told you how I run my business and given you insights into my beliefs regarding just about every area of business. From customer service to selling to leadership to teamwork and hiring and firing—you've got it now.

Just remember how simple it is, and don't complicate it!

Work hard.

Sell what you have—it won't sell itself.

Amaze the customer so well, he will want to do business with you over and over again and tell others about you.

Hire carefully.

Fire people quickly when it's necessary.

*Have fun and enjoy what you do, but most of all, do what
you are paid to do.*

Results are everything, and they never lie.

That's really about it.

So it comes down to this: Will this stuff work for you?
Beats me.

It might. It might not. It either absolutely will work for you
or absolutely won't work for you. That's how sure I am of this
stuff.

This is really all I know about accomplishing anything either
in life or in business: Stuff works only if you give it a try.

So give it a try. Pick one little thing that I've suggested and
see what you think. That's right, just one little thing. Don't lay
the book down and overhaul your whole business. That would
be overwhelming and would doom you to failure. Just try one
little thing. If it works, try one more little thing. If that works,
do it again. And on and on and on.

That's all I ask of you. I haven't suggested anything that is
really very hard. In fact, my original promise to you was that
this stuff would all be simple. I hope that now after reading the
book, you agree.

So stop now and look back through the book and pick out
your one thing. Then lay the book down and start. When? Today. Not tomorrow.

"This book is not to be tossed aside lightly. It is to be thrown with great force." —DOROTHY PARKER

Acknowledgments

Above all, I need to thank the businesses that have treated me badly, screwed me over, and taken advantage of me. Lousy treatment inspires me to fight back for myself and others in my writing, my speeches, and face-to-face.

Thanks to the idiots I worked for over the years who thought that being likable was more important than being competent or thought that being an asshole was a leadership style that would make me want to do a better job.

Thanks to all the employees who thought that getting the job *from* me was the only real work they would ever have to do *for* me.

Thanks to my superstar employees. You taught me to stay out of your way so you could get some real work done.

A special thank-you to the customers who ripped me a new one when I was stupid and pointed out what I could have done to serve them better. And to the customers who said no to me when I tried to sell them something, because in the rejection came the lesson on how to do better the next time.

Thank you to the authors and speakers who shared their

ideas through their books and speeches. You ticked me off, inspired me, and helped me clarify what made sense and what didn't.

I need to thank my wife, Rose Mary, who reins me in when I need it—which is most of the time. She is the regulating valve in my life and does a great job of keeping me in line.

To my sons, Tyler and Patrick, who remind me who I really am and keep me from getting too big for my britches. I also need to thank Vic Osteen, my friend and manager for more than a decade, who runs my life and my business so I don't have to. From the very beginning, he understood who I was and what I was trying to become better than any other person in my life.

To my editor, Erin Moore, and assistant editor, Jessica Sindler, who made this a better book by encouraging me to rewrite my ideas so you could understand them better. It wasn't always easy for any of us, but in the end, we all are winners because of their hard work.

To Bill Shinker, my publisher, who "got me" from the start. He took a chance on a mouthy self-help guy who knew some stuff about business and wanted to write a book about it.

To my literary agent, Jay Mandel of the William Morris Agency, for believing in me enough to invest the time to make all of this happen.

To Keppler Speakers, for their support and for keeping me in front of audiences around the world, spreading my philosophy of success.

This book is mine. If you like it, they get some of the credit; if you hate it, I'll take all of the blame.